Designing and Teaching an On-Line Course

Spinning Your Web Classroom

Heidi Schweizer
Marquette University

Allyn and Bacon
Boston · London · Toronto · Sydney · Tokyo · Singapore

Credits: Display 3B, page 33, is © 1997, H. Goodrich Andrade.
Marquette University logo used with permission of Marquette University.
Screen captures of LearningSpace® copyright © 1999 Lotus Development Corporation.
Used with permission of Lotus Development Corporation. LearningSpace is a registered
trademark of Lotus Development Corporation.

Copyright © 1999 by Allyn & Bacon
A Pearson Education Company
160 Gould Street
Needham Heights, Massachusetts 02494-2130

Internet: www.abacon.com

ISBN 0-205-30321-8

Printed in the United States of America

10 9 8 7 6 5 4   03 02 01 00

Contents

To:
Richard Schafer
Lauren Schafer

Acknowledgements

This adventure was not started alone; nor was it completed alone. From the conceptualization of the book to the final edit, I was supported, advised, encouraged and often inspired by family, friends, and colleagues without whom this book would still be in the "you really think I could write a book?" stage.

First and most importantly, I must acknowledge the love, support and awesome guidance my husband and best friend, **Dick Schafer**, provided. He, in his own right, is an experienced instructor and designer of distance learning courses. Dick consistently served as a limitless source of love, encouragement, creativity and scholarship.

I thank my daughter **Lauren**, eight years old, for putting up with mom "being on the computer all the time." She knew this book was important to me and was always able to wait while I finished up a chapter or refined a paragraph.

Mary Shuter, a dear friend and respected colleague worked side by side with me to complete this book. She is an awesome editor and a genuine friend. Mary's contributions to this book go beyond reviewing, editing, and revising. She was the graceful force that kept me on track, and in focus, always solving the seemingly unsolvable.

Martha Mealy, a true pioneer in the field of distance learning, is the Coordinator of the Instructional Technology Development Group for Learning Innovations–University of Wisconsin, Madison. Martha exemplifies what Henry Reyes, a student in one of my on-line courses, recently wrote:

> *"My father taught me as a child that things do not belong to you or me, they belong to those who need them most."*

Martha graciously, patiently and with genuine care, shared with me much of what she knew about distance learning and *LearningSpace*, the courseware package used throughout this book. Martha treated her vast knowledge and experience with distance learning as belonging to those of us who needed it most; a rare quality in this fast moving, highly competitive field.

Joan Whipp, a colleague at Marquette University and good friend, served as my own personal devil's advocate. She questioned assumptions, asked questions, and assumed nothing. Many of the illustrations used throughout the book were taken directly from a course in which she was the lead developer and on-line teacher. Joan's ability to critically reflect on her own practice and beliefs about teaching and learning helped me to become a much more thoughtful writer.

Nereus Dooley, a former student and now a colleague, served as a technical advisor over the past five months. He designed many of the screen captures used throughout the book. Most importantly, however, he never failed to listen as I worked through problems and always responded with practical suggestions.

Jill Purvis, another long time friend, worked hard to make this book copy-ready within some very tight deadlines. Her critical eye, organizational skills and amazing work ethic were essential throughout the process.

Lynn Welscher, a friend and colleague, served as the eagle-eye final copy editor. While working under extremely tight time constraints, Lynn fine-tuned the final copy, providing essential suggestions and insights.

Sally Captain, Administrative Assistant, School of Education, Marquette University, designed the Marquette University web pages used in the first chapters. Sally proved a highly capable web-master, an untiring and patient friend, and a source of encouragement and support throughout.

Finally, I thank the many, many people who patiently listened to me talk about this book, eagerly responded with creative and usable ideas and most importantly encouraged me to complete it.

This book now belongs to you.

De-Mystifying the On-line Environment

Educators in universities, technical schools, K-12 classrooms, corporations and training centers have leaped into the on-line world of distance learning and "virtual interaction." Over the past several years there has been an increase in the number of courses readily accessible on the Internet. In some ways, this leap was a leap of faith, as the early research and preliminary reports of what works and what doesn't in the on-line classroom are just now coming available. In other ways, it was a leap of joy as innovative and creative educators began to boldly explore the distance classroom and develop courses to meet the ever-growing need of both the traditional and non-traditional student. However you look at it, distance education is here and it is mushrooming. And, if you plan to join the rapidly growing ranks of distance education teachers, then you need to ask yourself the question, "how do I design and teach a successful on-line course?" Hopefully, you will find the answer to your question in this book.

A recent review of a variety of on-line courses, degree programs and certificate programs revealed that many on-line courses are poorly designed, pedagogically unsound, and amount to not much more than lecture notes or textbooks cut and pasted onto a Website. Up until recently, the unaware student consumer, in search of an on-line course, has been satisfied with "taking what I can get." That is, making uninformed decisions and choices related to the overall quality of the course in the rush to sign up for the convenience of an on-line degree. As more and more teachers enter their courses in the worldwide education marketplace, a standard for excellence and quality emerges.

This book explores the makings of a good on-line course. It is for the individual planning to develop and teach an on-line course; one that meets a high standard of quality. This book is intended to be a practical, applicable, hands-on-approach that takes both the novice and experienced on-line teacher through the steps of course development, on-line teaching, and on-line assessment. It includes designing a course that is outcome based, performance assessed, and collaborative. Learning theories such as Howard Gardner's Multiple Intelligences, William Glasser's Quality School and Roger and David Johnson's Cooperative Learning are also integrated in meaningful and practical ways. Actual examples from successfully developed on-line courses will be provided throughout to bridge the gap between theory and practice. A section entitled "It's Your Turn" gives the readers an opportunity to try out their skills at developing and teaching an on-line course. Finally, comments and insights from past on-line learners will be used throughout the book to address not just what the on-line course designer and teacher wants, but more importantly, what the on-line learner demands.

Selecting a Courseware Package

Designing and delivering a course on-line is made easy with the help of courseware. Courseware is software that is designed to deliver training or educational courses. Some of the courseware currently being used for course delivery are *Course in a Box*®, *First Class*®, *Top Class*®, and *LearningSpace*. This author selected *LearningSpace* as the product used to develop and teach the courses which are referred to throughout this book. *LearningSpace* is developed and distributed by Lotus Notes/IBM. This courseware product was chosen because it furnishes both the instructor and the student with an interactive, highly collaborative on-line learning environment that makes creating and teaching an on-line course obtainable to the "low-tech" teacher and student. Throughout this book you will see examples of screens captured from various on-line courses, developed in *LearningSpace*, to illustrate a point or clarify an application. As matter of fact, **Display 1A** shows me, Heidi Schweizer, the author of this book, just as I would appear to students who are about to begin my course on-line.

Display 1A

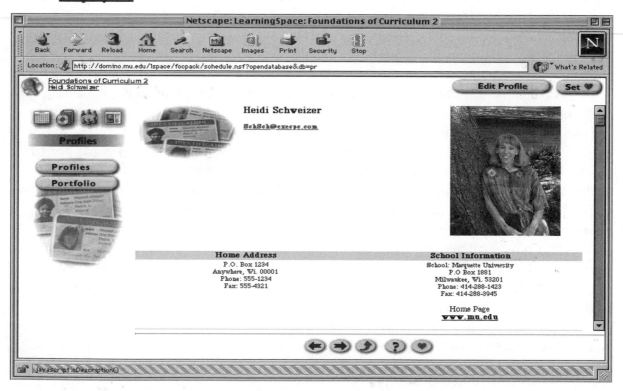

Navigating in *LearningSpace*

Since you will be viewing additional examples of screens from *LearningSpace* throughout this book, a conceptual understanding of how this product is designed and how both a student and instructor navigate *LearningSpace* may be helpful.

A useful metaphor to begin to conceptualize *LearningSpace* is to think of it as a school with only four rooms in which the students and the instructor work and interact. The four rooms are: The ScheduleRoom, the MediaCenter, the CourseRoom and the ProfileRoom. Each of these rooms has a special function and provide both the on-line student and instructor with a specific place "to go" to accomplish specific tasks. **Display 1B** shows a graphic of the four rooms.

Display 1B

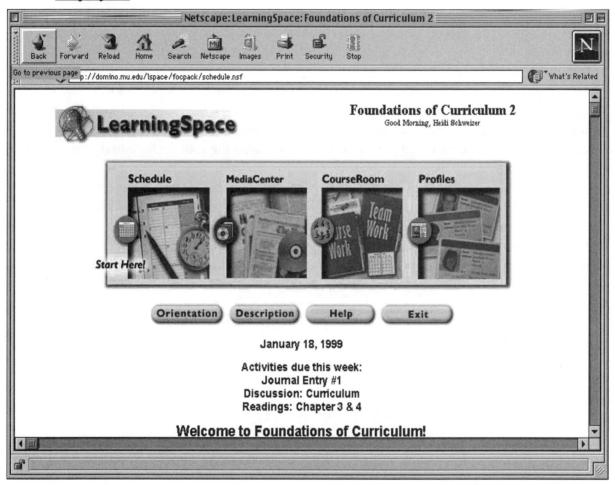

ScheduleRoom. The ScheduleRoom is the room where students go to find out about the class: what topics are taught, when the tests are administered, what readings are required, when assignments are due and the timeline for completion of the course. In addition, this is where the instructor posts course updates, special announcements, or changes to the course. The ScheduleRoom is often referred to as "home base" as it is where the student always begins when entering their on-line course.

ProfileRoom. The ProfileRoom is where both the students and the instructor go to "meet" other students enrolled in the course. The ProfileRoom lists all the names and e-mail addresses of fellow classmates and the instructors. In addition, each member of the class has their own "profile page" that could include a personal photograph as well as information about special interests, hobbies, and educational background. Much of this information asked for in this room is optional and up to each individual to decide how much they are comfortable with disclosing on-line. However, the ProfileRoom is a handy and friendly place to go to put a face with a name in an otherwise annonymous environment.

MediaCenter. The MediaCenter is where the instructor puts all the materials that support the course. It would be like the Instructional Media Center in a school or a library on campus. Materials that might appear in the MediaCenter include: lecture notes, PowerPoint® presentations, video clips, audio clips, photo collections, or web sites, to name a few. The instructor directs the student (from the ScheduleRoom) to "go to the MediaCenter" to view or listen to specific materials related to the unit or module being studied.

CourseRoom. The CourseRoom is similar to a traditional classroom in session. It is dynamic and interactive. It is where students and teachers are discussing a topic, reflecting on a reading, clarifying understandings, or raising questions. These discussions can occur in small groups, one-to-one or as a whole group. This is also the room where assignments are submitted for grading.

One final aspect of *LearningSpace* that is important, but does not have a specific room assigned to it, is that of assessment. *LearningSpace* provides the instructor with the tools to design and administer assessments on line (true/false, short answer, or multiple choice). *LearningSpace* also provides a student portfolio option where individual grades are recorded and instructor comments as to progress of an individual student are noted.

With this basic understanding of *LearningSpace* you are now ready to explore teaching and learning on-line!

Teaching in Cyberspace

Q: I am planning to put a course on-line. What do I do? How different will it be from a course offered in a face-to-face setting?

These questions are common for anyone who is about to enter into the frontier of on-line instruction. If you have questions about stepping into this new 'classroom,' do not worry. This book will help you answer your questions and prepare you for a successful venture into the field of on-line instruction. It will provide you with the strategies and tools you will need for teaching your course on-line.

As you prepare to take your course on-line, first consider the type of learning environment you will want to create for your students. You will want to establish an environment which encourages active learning as opposed to passive, rote learning. From your own personal experiences, you already know that as a student yourself, you enjoyed learning and got more out of a lesson or activity when you were encouraged to be an active participant in the learning process.

Interactive learning can take place in a variety of ways in an on-line classroom; between instructor and student, between student and the learning materials, among students, or between student and guest lecturer. It will be, however, your responsibility, as the instructor, to design a course that provides your students with these varied formats, and create a classroom that has an active, student-centered environment. This book will provide you with many suggestions and activities which will assist you as you design a meaningful, interactive, and successful on-line course for both you and your students.

Exchanging the classroom for a monitor and eye contact for a keyboard requires a major shift in our thinking about our role as both a teacher and course developer. We have all come to depend so much on a quizzical tip of the head or a sudden arm shooting into the air for clues as to how the lesson is going. Many of us have spent time after class re-explaining a concept or listening to a student's new idea. And, it is a rare teacher who has not, at the last minute, changed a lesson plan or added an activity to the day's instruction. So, how is it that we can be expected to teach in cyberspace when we can't watch our student's faces, capture the teachable moment on-line when our lesson is already planned, or be assured that our students are really learning, when we can not even hear their voices?

The answer is that it does work and has been working for many distance educators. What we have learned is that the successful distance educator knows their students, "not by their faces or their seat position in a vast lecture auditorium; but instead by the words and ideas they express in their weekly assignments"[1]And, that the student in cyberspace knows us, the teachers, not by our cheerful smiles and quirky styles, but by the individual and personal comments we make to them as they complete activities and engage in weekly discussions. There is no doubt about it, we have moved into a very different format for teaching and learning. But when we really think about it, teaching at a distance just reinforces what we have always believed about learning all along - that is, real education does not occur in a classroom or on a campus. It occurs in the minds of our students.

So, as we make this transition from "Sage on the Stage to Guide on the Side," let's look at how we can make our on-line classroom a place that is friendly, inviting, and optimizes learning.

The Quality On-line Classroom

Just as you consider creating a positive culture that supports and encourages learning in your face-to-face classroom, so must you consider creating such an environment for your on-line classroom.

Take a moment and think of a time when you had a memorable, meaningful learning experience. This could have been in school–like that time in your college statistics class when you finally understood standard deviation. Or, it could have been a learning experience outside of a formal school setting such as the time you were traveling in a foreign country and you developed a deeper understanding and appreciation for a culture different from your own.

Why was this experience such a valuable one? What happened to make it so memorable and meaningful for you?

Dr. William Glasser, a psychiatrist, educator, and philosopher who has been in the business of researching "learning" for the past 40 years has developed a research base for creating successful learning environments that he calls "Control Theory."[2] The essence of the research states that beyond the obvious physical needs that we all have, food, water, shelter, and so on, we also have four basic psychological needs that we are continually trying to fulfill. All of our behavior can be attributed to, in one degree or another, our efforts to make sure these four psychological needs are met. The research on control theory demonstrates that if we can create learning environments that are needs satisfying, then learning is optimized. The energy and attention that might be directed to fulfilling a psychological need can now be focused on learning. The four psychological needs are:

> *Belonging* - We all have a need to belong - the desire to connect with others, establish friendships, and to know that others care about us. It's being anti-lonely! Few of us would choose the life of a hermit. Much of our behavior is in search of love and belonging.

> *Freedom* - We all have a need to know that we can act and think without restriction by others. Freedom is being able to say "I choose to," "I want," "I will." Freedom is being able to make responsible choices.

> *Power* - The need for power is often misunderstood. It is not the need to control others. Instead, it is the need to know that others recognize you for what you do or say that is important and significant. Knowledge is power. You cannot do what you do not know. As you gain knowledge, you are capable of doing more things and you become more personally "empowered."

> *Fun* - We all have the need to simply laugh and feel good. We can accomplish this in a variety of ways. Successfully accomplishing a challenging task is fun. Being entertained is fun. We all know that when a learning situation is "fun" it is often more memorable and is much more likely to become a significant, meaningful learning experience. Learning situations that are not fun (i.e. boring, too easy, too hard) rapidly deteriorate into forgettable experiences.

Fulfilling Psychological Needs On-line

> *Q: How can I design an on-line classroom and make sure that these four psychological needs are addressed?*

Belonging

You need to think about creating a caring relationship with your students on-line just as you would do in a face-to-face classroom. Keep in mind that it is your job as a teacher to facilitate collaborative, supportive relations between your students as well as between you and your students. Following are a few suggestions on how to do that.

> - **Hold an on-site meeting.** If possible, bring the students to the university, school, campus or business site for an introductory face-to-face meeting, before you meet on-line. Repeating a face-to-face session halfway through the class and again at the end provides opportunities for students to reaffirm ties and "grow" personal relationships.

- **Introduce yourself on-line.** Provide a welcome letter and some background information about your experience, interests, family, and hobbies. The style of the letter should be informal and inviting, letting your students know that you are willing to share tidbits about your personal life. This begins to create a "human" connection that is essential to effective teaching. (See Appendix 1 for a sample introductory letter.)

- **Personalize your distance classroom.** Ask your students to complete a profile sheet that could include pictures, hobbies, interests, and information about their family or job. In *LearningSpace*, for example, there is a "room" labeled Profiles. In this room, students gain a sense of belonging through reading about classmates and finding common interests. It can be a convenient place to go to when involved in a discussion with a classmate, and a student is interested in knowing more about another student. **Display 1C** shows a sample Profile in *LearningSpace*.

- **Use cooperative learning.** Design opportunities for students to work together on assignments, discuss questions related to readings or complete projects. Establish cooperative groups so that each member is held accountable for contributing his or her fair share and the group functions in a "one for all and all for one" mode.

- **Be invitational.** Positive learning experiences are often described as knowing that the teacher cares about ME and will work just as hard as I do to ensure success. Make your on-line classroom friendly and open. Be accessible to your students–set clear office hours and adhere to them. Respond quickly to student concerns or requests.

- **Use electronic mail.** E-mail individual students who need extra support or encouragement. Learning on-line is a new experience for many students, therefore they can sometimes feel very threatened. Offer support and encouragement, particularly in the first few weeks of the class, for the student who is reluctant to venture on-line with his or her thoughts and ideas is essential. Assuring students that grammatical errors are okay when one is writing "conversational style" helps those who are sensitive about their extemporaneous writing skills to take a risk. Encouraging students to tackle the technical problems that on-line learning presents, creates a powerful sense of accomplishment when they are able to resolve them. And finally, be prepared to offer technical assistance to students when needed.

- **Be approachable, be personal.** Create an expectation that you are "there" for your students. Be open, willing to listen, and respectful of others ideas, concerns and frustrations. Responding quickly and thought

Display 1C

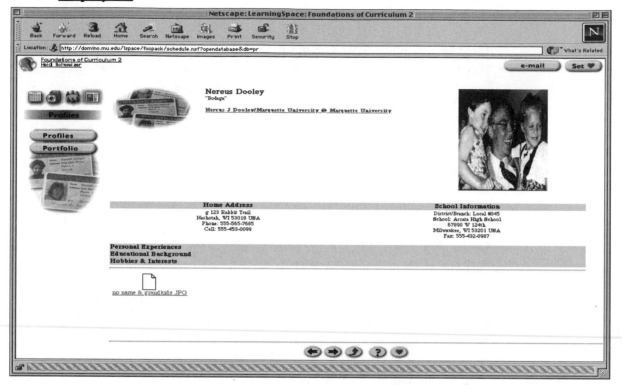

fully to student comments can not be over emphasized. As one seasoned distance learning student put it: "a good on-line instructor is one you don't have to wait until you are totally confused and frustrated to e-mail. Good instructors are the ones who write back and are prompt about answering questions." Make your course a place where ideas can be explored in a non-threatening, highly supportive environment that encourages risk-taking and creative problem solving."

Freedom

Meeting the need for freedom is easily accomplished on-line. By the very nature of asynchronous learning (students are not on-line at the same time), the students already can:

- make a choice of when and how they will complete an assignment.
- pace themselves to go faster or slower than others taking the course.
- choose, through electronic links, whether or not to explore a topic of particular interest in more depth.

As an instructor, you can design the class to provide for projects of the student's choice or options for completing assignments (make a web page, write a paper, do a PowerPoint® presentation).

Power

On-line learning is, by its very nature, empowering. Many of us have experienced the surge of power that comes when we have successfully manipulated technology to accomplish a task or goal. Learning on-line combines the satisfaction of mastering the use of a powerful tool (technology) with taking charge of one's own learning. Knowledge is power. We all are familiar with the example set by Jaime Escalante. Escalante, a Bolivian native, became an overnight celebrity when "Stand and Deliver" hit the theaters. The film chronicles his achievements at Garfield High School in East Los Angeles where he transformed a sub-standard math program into a nationally recognized program in which sixty percent of the calculus students passed Advanced Placement exams. Escalante accomplished these phenomenal results through great teaching, tough love, and empowering his students with the confidence to become successful. The more Escalante's students learned, the more powerful they became. Knowledge provides an incredible power base from which remarkable results will emerge. As an on-line instructor, keep the following tips in mind as you create an empowering on-line learning environment.

- Design learning experiences that are self-directed or that involve discovery learning. It is extremely empowering to tackle a problem, work through it and successfully complete it in a real, self-directed way.

- Create a variety of interactive learning experiences that allow students to share personal experiences related to the topic, as well as thoughts, questions and comments. Through interactive projects and discussions, each student is recognized by other students, and the instructor, as having made significant and valuable contributions.

- On-line learning becomes an empowering option for the student who is unwilling to speak up in class, takes longer to formulate an opinion or thought, or is reluctant to share an idea before hearing what others have said. On-line learning 'evens out' the playing field and allows the time and space for all voices to be heard.

Fun

On-line learning provides, at one's fingertips, a wide variety of resources and technologies that are fun and challenging to use. Ideas for creating a "fun" on-line environment include:

- Provide opportunities for tutorials, second chances, and enough time to master the material. If a student has a greater chance of successfully completing the course, he or she will leave the course with good feelings. Feeling successful is fun!

- Create interactive discussions and group work. Working on group projects and sharing in discussions on-line is fun. (Particularly for those students who hesitate to speak up in a face-to-face class or do not get a chance to because they are in a lecture hall with 500 other students).

- Open up opportunities for students to use their creative juices. Students are no longer constrained by the four walls of a lecture hall with bolted down seats, a chalk board in the front and no windows. Just think of the possibilities that an instructor and a student can create both on-line and off-line to markedly enhance the learning! The World Wide Web is at their finger tips. The information and insights gained can be shared immediately and becomes a dynamic resource for everyone in the class. Access to experts, through e-mail and web sites, becomes easier than walking to the front of the classroom and asking a teacher.

- Share the responsibility of posting a computer "joke of the week" with students in the class.

- Use an "Announcement" section of the course to update the class on upcoming events, course progress, interesting events and to extend holiday greetings.

- Create competition. Individual or group competition can add a dimension of excitement and fun that individual or cooperative work just does not seem to be able to do. If you are teaching an on-line geography course, for example, the following activity may create competition in your class-room. Tell your students that the first five who are able to find and post the Website that lists the three rainiest places on Earth will receive a personal cybergram from you. The incentive of a good challenge helps maintain a fun learning environment.

Final Hints

Many of your students will either be taking their first on-line course, or taking their first on-line course using your particular software package or delivery system. They are entering an entirely new learning environment that can be, at best, challenging and at worst, very threatening. It is important to recognize that before a student can be successful with the content and activities which you have provided in your on-line course, they must first be successful, or at least comfortable, with the process of learning on-line. Following are a number of ideas that could be used to introduce students to on-line learning that are fun, non-threatening and increase the likelihood of a successful experience:

- First teach how to get around or navigate the course. Don't assume that the course delivery packages (whether commercial or home-made) are intuitive and user friendly. Some instruction on how to move about the course, take part in discussions, access materials and submit projects and assignments is necessary. Make this process fun, non-threatening and valuable. Suggestions include:

√ Provide a printed version of the "on-line" help sections for easy reference.

√ Create simple, fun activities that teach students how to navigate your course. Examples include: on-line scavenger hunts to find different aspects of the course; a practice discussion where students pick a name for their on-line cooperative group; or an opportunity to take a "test" that is not graded.

√ If possible, require that the first class be a face-to-face meeting. Together, explore the course and answer technical and software concerns.

- Formal student support systems. As you send your students off into cyberspace with only their laptop and Netscape to help them navigate, you need to provide systematic, dependable and convenient "service stations" for them to "pull into" in case help is needed, a repair is warranted or a problem begins to emerge. For technical services, these "service stations" may take the form of an 800 number for 24 hour help; a help desk open from 7:00 a.m. until midnight, an every other day Saturday "bring your computer to campus day," or a guaranteed no more than 24 hour response time to any technical questions sent via e-mail or voice mail. In addition to technical assistance, students will need support in the following areas: registration, textbooks (purchasing and obtaining), grades, and the zillions of other questions that on-site students have about the courses they take, the programs they are in and the rules and regulations that govern them. It is important to assign a person to be responsible for "taking care of" the on-line student. The same strategies that work for technical assistance can work for all other questions that students have. The key is to anticipate the need and provide friendly, convenient, and useful answers.

- Ramp up. Design your beginning assignments to be technologically simple without sacrificing the rigor of the assignment. For example, have the first on-line discussion assignment be one in which the student is required to only post his or her comment. The next time, expect the student to post his or her comment and respond to one other. Later in the course, expect that a group of students engage in a lively cooperative group discussion. And, finally ask that an entire class (15 or less) respond to a question and engage in a discussion with a number of other students.

Similar "ramping up" procedures for submitting assignments, going to Web sites, activating PowerPoint® presentations, and viewing video-clips should be used. It is essential that you do not allow the technology to get in the way of learning. Teaching the technology, at least initially, is as important as teaching classroom procedures and protocol in a face-to-face setting.

- Encourage and support the traditional learner. The traditional learner who ventures into the on-line environment is immediately faced with adapting to two new situations. First, technology is now the medium for the delivery of instruction. And, secondly, being self-directed and self-disciplined become essential for success in a web-based learning environment.

Logging on to a server, using an internet browser and entering a course is sometimes frustrating and more time consuming than driving the 30 minutes to a local college campus to sit in a classroom. On the other hand, it often is not. Probably the single biggest complaint of on-line learners is the inconsistent or unreliable nature of technology. There is an erroneous notion out there that if it is "technical" it is better, faster, slicker and easier. Unfortunately the nature of technology is that it is forever changing and there will always be "glitches." As an instructor, you need to help your students understand that they need to take a "problem solving approach" to resolving their own technical glitches and connectivity problems. This will free them up to approach on-line learning as an exciting adventure rather than a major obstacle to overcome. On-line learners are truly pioneers and the successful ones will have the "pioneer spirit."

Summary

An on-line classroom needs to be fun, empowering, full of choices for students and a place where students feel that they "belong." When you create an on-line environment that meets these four basic psychological needs, you will create an environment where real LEARNING can take place.

On-line In-sites ...

In the Beginning, as students gear up to take their first on-line course, they realize they are entering an entirely new learning environment that can be, at best, challenging, and at worst, very threatening. These student comments provide an insight into the natural anxiety that exists when a new method is tried or a personal risk is taken.

- *Try and get on-line as often as possible to help ease the beginner's anxiety. The more you practice, the better you will feel about the course.*
- *Become as involved as possible as early in the course as possible. By that I mean, I think it would be wise to join the discussions and to become active in reading and responding to the comments of your fellow participants early in the semester. I procrastinated too much and I feel I missed a lot by not getting to know and sharing ideas with my classmates.*
- *Don't be afraid if you do not know how to use computers as well as others. I started taking the course without being as knowledgeable as some 'number one' computer experts. I found that I became as literate as some of them. I got rid of my fear of computers. I also found that the more you use the computer, the better you get.*
- *Communicating on-line was a new experience for me; I never participated in a chat room. I greatly missed the exchange of ideas that occurs in a traditional classroom. When I met my classmates at the very last class, I very much enjoyed the congenial atmosphere. I feel now that this congeniality may have been possible on-line if I had made greater effort. I think it would be worth the time it may take navigating the Learning Space to improve the congeniality of professional sharing. Be prepared to get excited, dive in and "just do it!" The ability to dialogue with others at a distance is motivation enough.*

 ## It's Your Turn!

Think about the course you are planning to offer on-line. What can you do to create an environment that will meet the four basic psychological needs: belonging, freedom, power, fun? One way you can get started is to write a welcome letter to your students. In this letter, provide some background information about your experience, interests, family and hobbies. In other words, personalize yourself, on-line. (See Appendix 1 for a sample Welcome Letter).

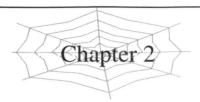

Guideline for On-line Course Development

Q: How do I begin to design my course for on-line learning? What do I put on-line and what do I leave out?

You now have a good idea of how you want your on-line classroom to look and feel. You are convinced an interactive, inviting and fun learning environment will produce the results you are expecting. Now it is time to explore in a very systematic and step-by-step approach, the process of planning and designing an on-line course. In many ways it is similar to the process you might use to design your face-to-face course. The significant difference, however, is the degree to which the instructor must plan and detail, in writing, all components of the course (outcomes, readings, activities, lecture notes, evaluations, etc.) prior to the first day of class.

Most of us are very familiar with distributing a course syllabus or course guide on the first day of our face-to-face class. In it we generally provide the student with a description of the course, overall course outcomes, the units to be covered, some of the readings to be used, projects to be completed and the exam dates. What we most likely have not finalized at that point are the exact questions for the midterm and final, all of our lecture notes, an exhaustive list of readings, or even the various discussion questions we plan to introduce. Typically, as the semester progresses, we finalize the course as additional readings are added, "lectures" are created, activities are designed, classroom discussion questions are developed and test questions are constructed. We simply do not prepare every aspect of an entire course prior to the first day of class; especially if it is the first time we have taught the course.

The planning and design of an on-line course requires us to strike a unique balance between a course that is highly structured and detailed prior to the first day of class, with the need to retain flexibility and spontaneity as it relates to both teaching and learning. The on-line student needs to experience a course that is well designed, permitting he or she to navigate through it with little confusion and gain a clear sense of what is expected. And, that same on-line student also needs to know that there is always room for exploring the unexpected; raising unanticipated questions or following an unforeseen learning path. Similarly, the on-line instructor needs to be able to make full use of "the teachable moment" while maintaining a learning environment that is focused, rigorous and worthwhile.

Creating an on-line learning environment, where learning and success are the norms and collaboration and self-directed learning are the methods, is the goal. A Performance Based Model for Curriculum Design and Assessment is the means by which that goal can be reached.

The Foundation: Performance Based Curriculum Design

Performance Based Curriculum Design is a model for curriculum development that focuses on organizing an instructional effort (program, course, unit) around clearly defined outcomes that we want all students to demonstrate when they have completed the instructional unit, course or program. An **outcome** is defined as the knowledge, skill or affect to be developed by learners as a result of active participation in a planned learning experience. Comprehensive planning that is focused on clearly defined performance outcomes has a positive effect on student learning and achievement. Unfortunately, most teachers focus on activities and tasks as the basis for planning instructional units. Shifting our thinking to **first** deciding what it is we want our students to know or be able to do when they finish our course and **then** looking at the activities and tasks that will make the learning meaningful, fun and relevant is critical to successful on-line teaching and learning.

Overview of Performance Based Curriculum Design

Performance Based Curriculum design relies on clearly defined learner outcomes at three different levels: **Program**, **Course** and **Unit**. Each of these will be explained in detail later. However, in the spirit of clarity and simplicity, it is necessary to provide a common definition of the following terms that will be used throughout this chapter.

Glossary

- *Program*: A group of courses or units of instruction, which build toward a final goal(s). Often a Program will end in a degree, certification, meeting a graduation requirement or diploma.

- *Program Description*: A one or two paragraph description of a program - usually in an easy to read, narrative format.

- *Course Description*: A one or two paragraph description of a single course - usually in an easy to read, narrative format.

- *Culminating Program Outcomes*: Written at the *PROGRAM* level and defines the exit competencies expected of the learner upon completing the entire program. Culminating Program Outcomes are the ultimate synthesis and application of all prior learning.

- *Culminating Course Outcomes*: Written at the *COURSE* level and defines what it is we want the student to know and be able to do upon completing the course. Course outcomes represent a demonstration, synthesis and application of knowledge and skills gained in the course.

- ***Unit Outcomes***: Written at the *UNIT* or *MODULE* level and defines, in more detail, the essential components of knowledge and skills upon which both the program and course culminating outcomes ultimately depend.

The power of Peformance Based Curriculum Design depends on the degree of alignment between the Culminating Program Outcomes, Culminating Course Outcomes and Unit Outcomes. The stronger the alignment, the more powerful the program becomes and the higher the level of student success. A direct alignment between what we want students to know and be able to do upon exiting our program, the outcomes we designate for each course and the enabling outcomes we teach within each unit of each course, creates a success loaded on-line learning environment.

Display 2A illustrates the relationship between Culminating Program Outcomes, Culminating Course Outcomes, and Unit Outcomes in a well-aligned curriculum.

Display 2A

Culminating Program Outcomes		
Course A **Culminating Outcomes**	**Course B** **Culminating Outcomes**	**Course C** **Culminating Outcomes**
Unit 1 Outcomes	Unit 1 Outcomes	Unit 1 Outcomes
Unit 2 Outcomes	Unit 2 Outcomes	Unit 2 Outcomes
Unit 3 Outcomes	Unit 3 Outcomes	Unit 3 Outcomes

Designing Down

How do we begin thinking about what it is we want our students to know and be able to do when they finish our on-line course? How do we stop asking ourselves "How am I going to teach this topic" and instead ask ourselves "What are my students going to learn ..."?

William Spady, an educator and researcher who has devoted his career to the development of a curriculum model that focuses on student outcomes, clearly defines the process of shifting our thinking when he writes:

> ... start at the end point–with your intended outcomes–and define, derive, develop, and organize all your curriculum designing and instructional planning, teaching,and assessment on those desired demonstrations. Veteran practitioners call this the DESIGN DOWN or 'design back from the end' process. Often one hears design down from where you want to end up.[3]

The following sections in this chapter provide a systematic, step-by-step approach to planning and designing your on-line **course** within the larger framework of a **program**. Guidelines and examples for writing **Program** and **Course Descriptions**, **Culminating Program Outcomes**, **Culminating Course Outcomes** and **Unit Level Outcomes** will be provided.

Program and Course Descriptions. We have all been asked to write a one or two paragraph description of a program we offer or a course we teach. A **program description** describes, in summary form, the scope of an entire program–not just one course. A **course description**, on the other hand, describes one particular course. Both program and course descriptions are often used in college bulletins, staff development handbooks, and training manuals as a way of introducing a student to a learning opportunity. They both are simple statements that describe what the program or course intends to do. They give direction, set the tone and establish the priorities in an easy to read narrative format.

Program and course descriptions usually appear both on-line and in a print version of a student handbook for the program. An example of an on-line program description and course description are provided in **Display 2B** and **Display 2C**.

Display 2B

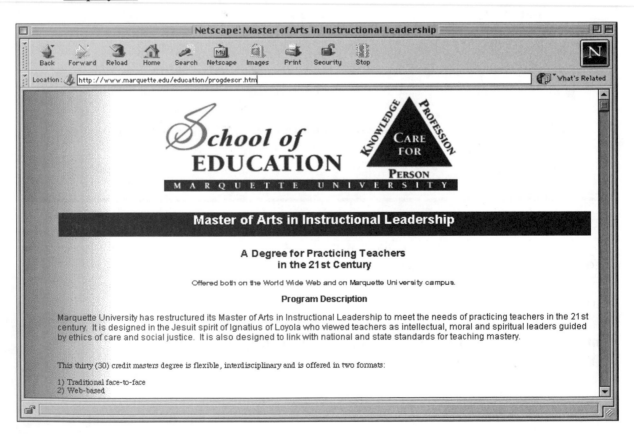

Display 2C

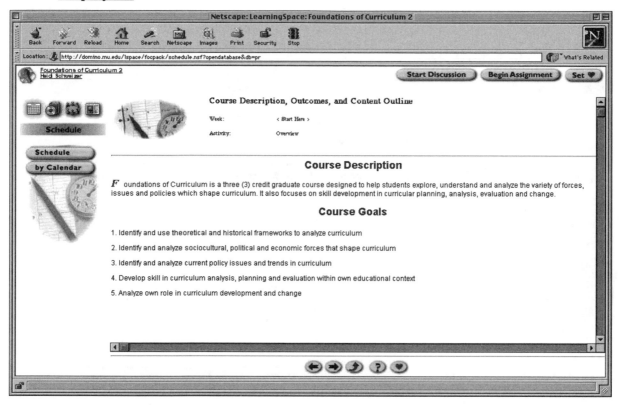

Culminating Program Outcomes. Designing a course for on-line delivery requires us to clearly define student outcomes at potentially three different levels: program, course and unit. The outcomes defined at the Program level are called Culminating Program Outcomes.

Culminating Program Outcomes define the scope and intended breadth of an entire program; not just a single course. For example *"The Theory and Design of Curriculum,"* and *"Using Technology for Instruction and Assessment,"* are two courses within a ten course sequence that make up a Master's Program in Instructional Leadership. Or, the typical sequence of high school math courses, required in high schools across the nation for graduation, are all part of a district's overall Math Program. Most courses do not stand alone. They are, instead, part of a larger array of courses leading to a degree, certificate or diploma.

Culminating Program Outcomes need to be clearly written and easily accessible to the on-line student. Typically, in an on-line course, they will appear on the Web page designated for the program being offered which is also often linked to the university, college, or institution's homepage. In addition, the Culminating Program Outcomes should be provided in print format in a student document that provides all relevant information about the program. An example of the Culminating Program Outcomes for a Masters Degree in Instructional Leadership as they appear on a University Homepage are illustrated in **Display 2D**.

Display 2D

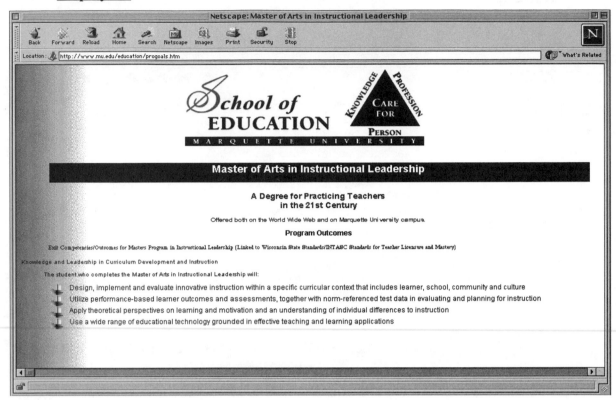

Culminating Course Outcomes. Culminating Course Outcomes define the expectations for one particular course. They are specific to the course, and also directly related to some, if not all, of the Culminating Program Outcomes. Culminating Course Outcomes are usually stated at the beginning of the course to provide the student with a clear idea of what is to be expected. An example of the Culminating Course Outcomes for one of the courses in the Masters Degree in Instructional Leadership, *"Foundations of Curriculum,"* is provided in **Display 2E**.

Unit Level Outcomes. Unit Level Outcomes are the essential components of knowledge and skills upon which both the program and course culminating outcomes ultimately depend. They are the expectations you have as the instructor for what it is you want the learner to know and be able to do as a result of experiencing a particular unit of instruction. And, they are just as essential to the learners as they enable them to successfully build the skills and knowledge to demonstrate mastery of the culminating course and program outcomes. A metaphor that might bring clarity and focus to the important role that unit level outcomes play is to think in terms of a journey. As the learner sets out on an adventure by foot across a varied and interesting landscape, the unit level outcomes become the small stepping stones that enable the learner to cross the creek (course). They become the footholds in the side of a hill (course) that enable the learner to reach the top. And they become the roots that offer a handhold down a slippery slope (course) toward the journey's end (program).   Unit level outcomes enable the learner to achieve the culminating course outcomes.

Display 2E

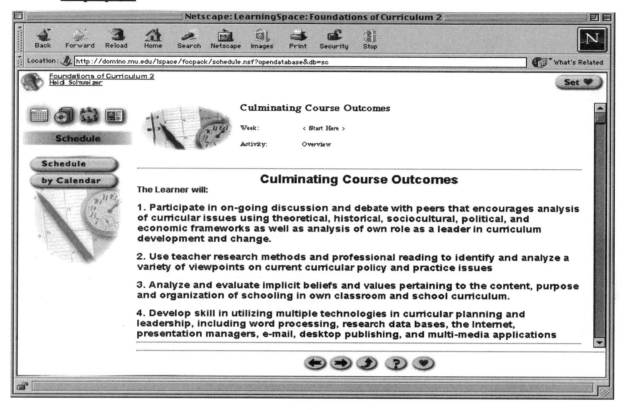

Unit level outcomes require carefully chosen verbs and significant content. They differ from course and program outcomes in that they relate directly and specifically to a small "chunk" of a course; and, not all unit level outcomes are assessed at the unit level. An example of unit level outcomes in an on-line course are illustrated **Display 2F**.

Whatever the program, course or unit to be developed, all need clearly defined student outcomes to guide the on-line learner. Opportunities to clarify, remind, re-state, or re-explain are limited in the on-line environment so letting the student know exactly what is expected is essential.

Writing Student Outcomes

Writing outcomes, whether they are at the program, course or unit level, require you as the course designer and instructor to identify what it is you expect the student to demonstrate, not what is to be taught, and then to write the expectations in terms of student demonstrations. You are organizing the course around the LEARNER, not the TEACHER. The VERBS that you choose to use in your outcomes set the stage for the level of rigor, complexity and higher order thinking you expect from your students. Therefore, it is important to select your verbs carefully! If your outcome is: *the student will be able to LIST (the verb!) the three major causes of the Civil War*, then the simple task of memorizing the three major causes of the Civil War and listing them for you on a written exam is acceptable. However, if

Display 2F

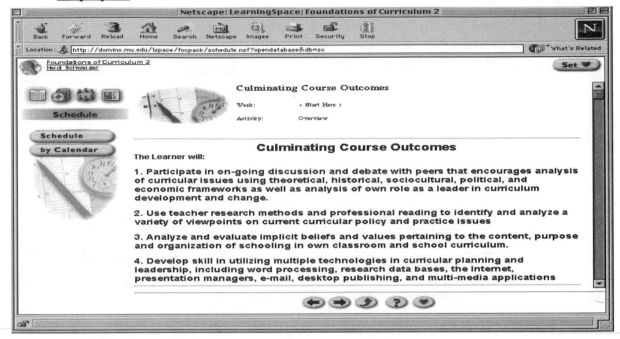

you choose more powerful verbs such as: *the student will EXPLAIN in his/her own words the major causes of the Civil War and then DESCRIBE to fellow group members, how these causes could be similar to a situation in his or her own life resulting in a personal "civil war,"* the standards are immediately raised. A deeper understanding of the causes of the Civil War is expected and the ability to apply that understanding in a completely different context is required. This becomes a much more rigorous expectation resulting in the student demonstrating his or her mastery of the subject in a very complex and comprehensive way.

A second aspect of writing a good performance based outcome is asking yourself, "is this outcome significant"? or, stated differently, "does this outcome *contribute* to the student being able to face future challenges and opportunities in a meaningful and significant way"? We all teach a lot of things that we find hard pressed to defend when a student asks, "so why is this so important to learn"? If we are not convinced that we have a believable answer to that question, perhaps we need to look at what we are asking the student to learn. Memoriz-ing the 50 state capitals may win us a few Jeopardy points, but how often have we been stopped on the street and asked to name the capital of Iowa? When designing your outcomes for your program, course or unit, think carefully and long about the relevance, applicability and meaningfulness of what you are expecting the student to learn.   In the course entitled, *"Using Technology for Instruction and Assessment,"* teachers were expected to become technology leaders in their respective schools. In preparation for this, they needed a solid understanding of the technical resources available to them in their individual buildings. An outcome of significance, written for this course was:

The teacher will evaluate technological resources available for instruction and assessment to both faculty and students in their building in relation to equity concerns (access, attitudes, available training) and suggest strategies for improvement.

Finally, the third dimension of a good outcome is the context in which you expect the student to demonstrate his or her mastery of the outcome. In the previous example, where we asked the student to be able to *list* three causes of the Civil War, the context for demonstrating mastery is a written quiz or test. In the example where we asked the student to *explain* the causes of the Civil War in his own words and then *describe* it to fellow group members, the context becomes a "live" interaction between two students discussing a personal experience. As a result, the context becomes more authentic, making the outcome more meaningful, memorable and sustainable. Creating outcomes that have an authentic context for demonstration expands the opportunities for real learning to take place.

Bloom's Taxonomy

Benjamin Bloom, an educational psychologist, created a handy hierarchy of VERBS from which to select when deciding on the level of complexity for the outcomes we write. It is entitled "Bloom's Taxonomy" and it provides us with six levels of complexity and examples of verbs for each level. The six levels are:

- **Knowledge**: appropriate when we expect the student to recall information, remember specific terminology and facts

- **Comprehension**: appropriate when we expect the student to summarize or explain in own words, translate materials and ideas, and predict immediate implications or effects on the basis of known facts

- **Application**: appropriate when we expect the student to use the information in its original or a new form

- **Analysis**: appropriate when we expect the student to predict an outcome, generalize, or breakdown an idea, principle, rule or fact into its element parts, recognize unstated assumptions, and check for consistency

- **Synthesis**: appropriate when we expect the student take information from a single body of knowledge or from several bodies of knowledge to form a new whole

- **Evaluation**: appropriate when we expect the student to make a judgment and support the judgment with a coherent rationale or to assess the value of something using specific criteria

When writing outcomes, think carefully about the verbs you choose. Outcomes that use beginning level verbs are appropriate in many instances. However, expecting your students to go beyond the simple "recall" level adds to the power and quality of your unit, course or program and raises the expectations for all your students.

Bloom's Taxonomy is reproduced for your use in Appendix 2 of this book. It is an invaluable tool when designing courses as it provides a quick and easy reference to verbs of significance.

Writing the Course Outline

A Course Outline is simply a visual organizer for the student. It provides, at a glance, a quick overview of the main units of study in the course. Underneath each of the main units is a more detailed listing of the major subpoints in the unit.

Once the outline is prepared, the class schedule can be written. The class schedule provides the student with a time organizer. It is displayed for students, in a calendar format and clearly lays out when a unit is to begin and end, as well as the assignments due for that unit. Some courses may be designed to be more flexible and fluid in the delivery. For example, there may be no timelines for the completion of one unit before the next one begins. If that is the case for your course, the class schedule is still a valuable organizer for the on-line student, but would just not include specific timelines. Examples of both a **Content Outline** and **Class Schedule** are provided **Display 2G** and **Display 2H**.

Display 2G

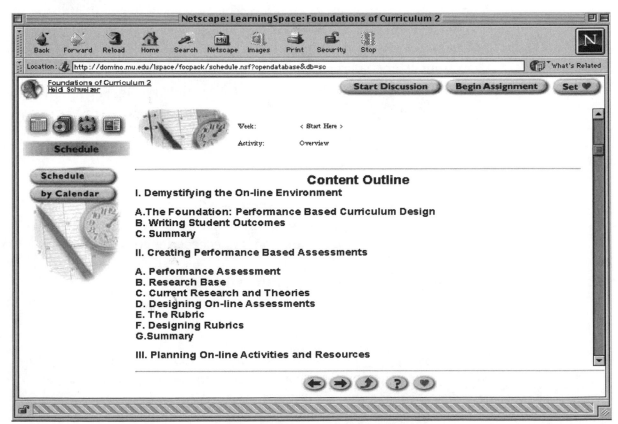

Display 2H

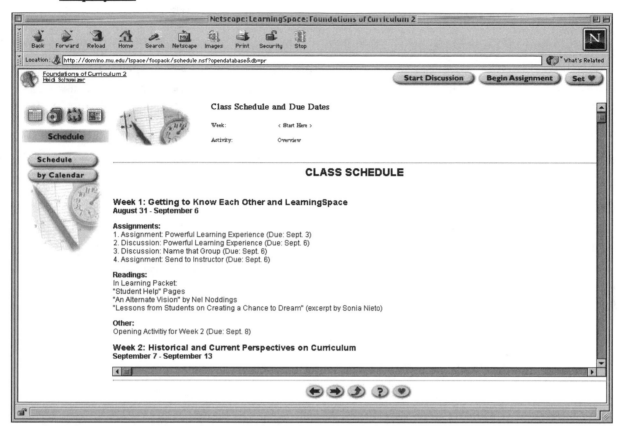

Summary

Performance based curriculum design is a model for curriculum development that focuses on organizing an instructional effort around clearly defined outcomes that we expect all students to demonstrate upon completion of the instructional unit. Outcomes are defined as the knowledge, skill or affect to be developed by the learner as a result of active participation in a planned learning experience. These outcomes can be written at a basic level or at higher levels that require the learner to apply, synthesize or evaluate information. It now becomes our challenge, as the creators of web-based courses, to FIRST formulate, in very clear and challenging terms, what it is we expect our students to know and be able to do by the end of our course. Only after we have created this focus (outcomes) for the student (and instructor) should we begin to formalize the activities, resources and tasks that will engage the student in mastering the outcomes. We all know creative teachers are always coming up with interesting activities and projects for the courses they teach. And, it is only natural that as we write outcomes for our course, ideas for great resources, fun activities and inspiring questions constantly come to mind. That's okay! Jot the ideas down for later use. Finalize your outcomes and then review your activity ideas to determine if they are appropriate. Some may be and some may not be, depending on the decisions you make regarding program, course and unit outcomes.

The planning and preparation that goes into designing a performance based course for delivery on the World Wide Web often involves a considerable time commitment. The alignment of unit, course and program outcomes requires thoughtful decisions and frequent revisions of what it is we REALLY expect our students to learn. Writing outcomes is not as much fun as creating clever activities and locating powerful web-sites to support our content. However, when your course is done, and it is presented to your on-line students, be assured that your students will find a course designed with the learner in mind that provides a challenging, focused, meaningful learning environment.

 It's Your Turn!

What is it you would like your students to know or be able to do upon completion of your on-line course? Where does your course 'fit in' with other courses offered in the program? Use this activity to begin writing outcomes for the **Program**, **Course** and **Unit Levels** of the course you want to teach on-line.

2.1.   **Name of your course:**_____

2.2.   **Write a brief PROGRAM description (summarize the scope of the program in which your course belongs):**

2.3.   **Write the CULMINATING PROGRAM OUTCOMES:**

2.4   **Write a brief COURSE description:**

2.5.   **Write the CULMINATING COURSE OUTCOMES:**

2.6.   **Select one or two units for this course. Write the UNIT LEVEL OUTCOMES for each of these units.**

Creating Performance Based Assessments

– by Heidi Schweizer with Joan L. Whipp[4]

Q: How will I know if my students are learning? How will I know my students are doing the work? How do I know my students can apply what they are learning?

Performance Assessment

The answer to all three questions above is performance assessment. Performance assessment is defined as the use of clearly defined criteria (rubric) to assess a student's ability to APPLY the knowledge and/or skills he or she has learned in an observable and measurable demonstration. An observable and measurable demonstration can take many forms: writing assignments, speeches, portfolios, simulations, contests/games, or dramatic presentations, to name just a few. A performance assessment is rarely, if ever, a paper and pencil test with multiple choice responses or true and false options. Performance assessment requires the student to apply the skills and knowledge gained to something personal, meaningful and applicable in his or her life. In the process of converting knowledge to a meaningful application, the student develops a much deeper understanding of the content, as well as a useful connection to the "real world."

Research Base

Traditionally, assessment was looked at as coming at the end of teaching and learning–the test on Friday or the test six weeks from now. Teaching was seen as a process of covering material and pouring information into a student's head. Learning was seen as taking in information and facts and memorizing them for a test.

During the last ten years, however, there has been an explosion in research about the brain and how people learn. Constructivist and multiple intelligence learning theories, including research on the brain, are helping us better understand how people learn, how people need to be taught and the role that assessment needs to play in the learning process.

Current Research and Theories on Learning and Assessment

Constructivism

Constructivist theory draws from a variety of psychological and philosophical perspectives, including those of J. Piaget, J. S. Bruner, L. Vygotsky, and J. Dewey.

Constructivist theory is based on the idea that knowledge exists within each of us; and that we as learners actively construct knowledge as we attempt to make sense of our experiences.

As learners attempt to create meaning, they construct mental structures, models, or what Piaget called "schema." As the learner encounters new experiences, particularly those which do not fit already formed structures, the learner revises his or her mental model to "accommodate" the new experiences. Vygotsky and his followers stress that this active construction of meaning occurs in a social context. The learner negotiates meaning and tests understandings with teachers, mentors, or more knowledgeable peers.

Multiple Intelligence Theory

Howard Gardner's multiple intelligence theory compliments constructivist theory in that it suggests multiple ways that learners can represent their learning. Gardner argues that traditional paper and pencil tests and standardized intelligence tests only measure two types of intelligence: logical-mathematical and verbal. There are, however, many people who have great capacities for learning in other ways. For example, there are people who are highly gifted musically or who learn best spatially or through interpersonal relationships. Gardner argues that there are many kinds of intelligence and that schools and teachers must work to develop multidimensional assessments that include attention to visual, auditory, kinesthetic, intrapersonal, interpersonal as well as verbal and logical-mathematical abilities and skills.

A more detailed list and explanation of the many different types of intelligences and how they can be addressed in an on-line course is provided in Chapter Four: "Planning On-line Activities."

Brain-Based Research

Research on the brain has offered a more sophisticated understanding of the brain's plasticity and complexity and how the brain's anatomy affects attention and memory. New understandings of how the brain operates suggests that learning is maximized in rich and complex learning environments which offer multiple opportunities for hands-on learning, dialogue with others, making connections across disciplines and various forms of expression.

Summary of Research and Theories on Learning and Teaching: Implications for Assessment

What have we learned from the extensive body of research regarding learning and assessment? How can we apply what we now know to constructing assessments for on-line courses?

We have learned:

- Learners need a complex, activity-rich learning environment which arouses interest, curiosity, and offers multiple ways to make meaning. Instruction and assessment must respond to the brain's natural inclination to see patterns, make connections and create.
- Learning and instruction must always be connected to what the learner already knows.
- Learning is a social activity. Teachers need to maximize opportunities for students to negotiate meanings in real life, to communicate and test understanding with and against that of others.
- Learners must be given the opportunity, whenever possible, to demonstrate their learning in authentic contexts. Learners need performance-based instruction and assessment.
- Rather than the traditional paper and pencil test at the end of a lesson or unit, assessment should be ongoing. Throughout the learning process multiple assessments should be used to give meaningful feedback to both teacher and learner about what is being learned.
- Assessments should tap into multiple intelligences so that all students have ample opportunity to show what and how much they know. Teachers should use a variety of assessments that allow for visual, kinesthetic, musical, interpersonal, intrapersonal, logical-mathematical and verbal forms of expression.
- Students should have access to models of good performances.

With a fundamental background in learning and assessment theory, it is now time to create another link in your curriculum design process: the alignment of your assessments with your Culminating Course Outcomes. You now need to ask yourself: "what kind of things can I expect my students to do to demonstrate to me that they have indeed mastered my course outcomes?"

Designing On-line Assessments

At this point you have already identified learner outcomes at the program, course and unit levels. Now you are ready to design assessments that allows the student to SHOW you that he or she has mastered the Culminating Course Outcomes you have so clearly laid out for them. Another term frequently used for this type of assessment is **summative assessment**. Summative assessments are the demonstrations of learning you expect at the **end of a course or program**. For the purposes of this chapter, we will use the term Performance Based Assessment.

A very simple and straightforward example of a performance based assessment which is perfectly aligned with the course outcomes is illustrated in an activity that occurs every day across the nation to the delight of 14-16 year olds: Learning to drive so one can obtain a driver's license. The performance based outcomes for a driver's education course might be (1) *The student will be able to apply the laws and rules that govern safe driving (speed limits and signs) to hypothetical situations. (2) The student will be able to successfully pass a road test that involves starting the car, shifting gears, changing lanes, parking the car and turning the car off.* The performance assessments for these outcomes would include both a written test that poses hypothetical situations related to road signs and speed limits, and a driving test where the student actually demonstrates his/her ability to safely drive. A clearly defined rubric that spells out what the students must successfully do during the driving test adds to the overall learning experience. An example of how this rubric might look appears in **Display 3A.**

When planning assessments for on-line courses, it is important to think creatively and "out of the box." This is the time to provide a wide range of opportunities for students to tap into their own "intelligences." Projects can be created or PowerPoint® presentations can be substituted for a research paper; both different ways for the student to demonstrate the mastery of the same content or skill. The on-line student can mail, fax, e-mail or drop off in your office their final "demonstration."

Following are a few examples of assessments that instructors have used in their on-line courses that address Howard Gardner's Multiple Intelligences:

- In an instructional unit on drug abuse: A PowerPoint® presentation that explains the harmful effects of drugs on the body (visual/spatial, musical (sound effects)

- In a science unit: An animation project that shows a volcanic eruption (visual, logical/mathematical)

- In a social studies program that expected students to become actively involved in their community: A letter written to a senator stating why gun control legislation is necessary (linguistic)

- In a language arts program which stressed communication skills: A video-tape that demonstrated the skills needed for public speaking (linguistic, body-kinesthetic, interpersonal)

- In an architectural design course: A CAD project that demonstrates understanding of spatial relationships, accuracy and creativity (logical/mathematical, visual/spatial)

- In an integrated science and social studies unit: A Sim City® project that shows the interrelationships between industrial progress, community living and maintaining a healthy environment. (Intrapersonal, interpersonal, spatial, logical/mathematical)

Display 3A

Criteria		Quality		
Rules and Laws	Given a situation, three correct decisions are made and two laws are appropriately applied.	Given a situation, all but one decision is correctly made and all laws are appropriately applied.	Given a situation, more than one decision and one of the laws is missed.	Given a situation, all the decisions are incorrect and both of the laws are incorrectly applied.
Start the Car	Correctly does the following: adjusts seat, mirror, puts on safety belt and successfully turns the ignition key.	Thee of the four criteria are met.	Two of the four criteria are met.	Less than two of the four criteria are met.
Shift Gears	The following actions occur: • Identified the appropriate time to shift gears • Depresses clutch and smoothly shift to the appropriate gear • Smoothly releases clutch and proceeds with no jerking • Observes other cars as gears are shifted	Three of the four criteria are met.	Two of the four criteria are met.	Less than two of the four criteria are met.
Change Lanes	The following conditions are met: • Observes traffic to ensure that a lanes change is safe • Signals at appropriate time • Changes lanes in a timely fashion • Adheres to the speed limits • Adheres to the laws governing lane changes	Four of the five criteria are met.	Three of the five criteria are met.	Less than three of the five criteria are met.
Parallel Park	The following conditions are met: • Approaches parking space with care; always observing traffic • Pulls a half a car length in front of the front vehicle • Backs into space without touching either car or the curb • Pulls forward to center car in space	Three of the four criteria are met.	Two of the four criteria are met.	Less than two of the four criteria are met.

The Rubric

The final component for designing a powerful assessment is a rubric. A rubric is a scoring tool that lists the criteria for a piece of work, or the major points on which the student will be graded. For example, eye contact, strong voice, clear beginning, middle and end, and neat/clean in appearance are some criteria required for a public speaking performance. Or, a rubric for an e-mail project could include criteria for spelling and grammatical expectations, clearly defined purpose and supporting paragraphs, socially acceptable on-line behavior, and so on. As stated in an article by Heidi Goodrich:

> Rubrics appeal to teachers and students for many reasons. First they are powerful tools for both teaching and assessment. Rubrics can improve student performance, as well as monitor it, by making teachers expectations clear and by showing students how to meet these expectations. The result is often marked improvements in the quality of student work and in learning. A second reason rubrics are useful is that they help students become more thoughtful judges of the quality of their own and others work........... Third, rubrics reduce the amount of time teachers spend evaluating student work. ...... When the teacher does have something to say, he/she can often simply circle an item in the rubric, rather than struggling to explain the flaw or strength they have noticed. Rubrics provide students with more informative feedback about their strengths and areas in need of improvement............ Finally, rubrics are easy to use and explain.[5]

A rubric is a useful tool that not only shows you, the instructor, if the student is learning, but provides the student with yet another meaningful learning experience. The more specific and detailed the rubric, the clearer it is for the student. For example, in **Display 3B**, it is important to note that words such as "creative" and "boring" can be problematic as they can mean different things to different people. Specifically stating what is meant by "creative" (i.e. uses visuals, theatrics, music, or other unique approaches to gain student's attention) makes the instructors expectations clear and dimishes the likelyhood of a student misunderstanding or making false assumptions.

Rubrics can take many forms from a simple checklist to a detailed analysis (with accompanying point values) of each and every component of a successful demonstration. The rubric can be developed by the instructor or cooperatively with the students. **Display 3B** and **Display 3C** are two examples of rubrics.

Designing Rubrics

Writing a rubric for the first time can be difficult. However, once you have successfully completed one or two, it becomes increasingly easy and begins to require less and less time. There are, however, a few tips for writing good rubrics:

Display 3B

Criteria		Quality	
Did I get my audience's attention?	Creative beginning	Boring beginning	No beginning
Did I tell what kind of book?	Tells exactly what type of book it is	No sure, not clear	Didn't mention it
Did I tell something about the main character?	Included facts about character	Slid over character	Did not tell anything about main character
Did I mention the setting?	Tells when and where story takes place	Not sure, not clear	Didn't mention setting
Did I tell one interesting part?	Made it sound interesting --I want to buy it	Told part and skipped on to something else	Forgot to do it
Did I tell who might like the book?	Did tell	Skipped over it	Forgot to tell
How did I look?	Hair combed, neat, clean clothes, smiled, looked up, happy	Lazy look	Just got-out-of-bed, head down
How did I sound?	Clear, strong, cheerful voice	No expression in voice	Difficult to understand-- 6 inch voice or screening

Adapted from *Understanding Rubrics*, by Heidi Goodrich, Educational Leadership, May 1992

Display 3C

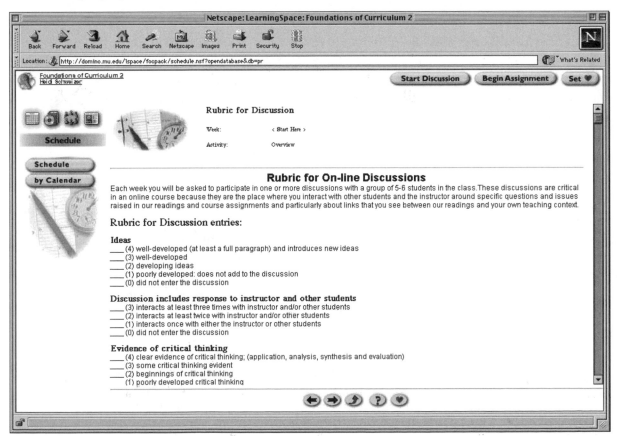

- Review your outcomes and make certain that what you are asking your students to do in the assessment is congruent with your outcomes.

- Brainstorm a variety of ways students will be able to demonstrate their mastery of the outcome. Don't get stuck on requiring the traditional paper or book report for demonstration. Take into consideration the opportunities the ever-growing field of technology brings to student assessment.

- After deciding on the "context" of the demonstration, list the criteria for what you think counts for quality work.

- Break the criteria into distinct categories.
  - Describe what constitutes a "quality" effort in each category.
  - Then describe what constitutes an "OK" effort in each category.
  - Third, describe what constitutes a "below average" effort in each category.
  - And finally, describe what constitutes a "failing effort" in each category.

- Check to be sure that the language you have used is clear and concise and will not be misinterpreted or misunderstood.

- Avoid unnecessary negative language. We all respond better to being told what is working and how we can improve than we do to what is wrong.

- Always give the rubric to the student prior to the assessment.[6]

Creating the rubric is the hard part, using them is the fun part. Once they are created they can be used over and over again, reducing the time involved in evaluation and assessment. (See Appendix 3 for a sample rubric.)

Unit Level Assessment

Often times, informal assessment (also called formative assessment), takes the place of more formal assessments at the unit level.   Formative assessments can occur throughout a course and provide both the instructor and learners valuable information as to progress being made. When formative assessments disclose that students are having difficulty, opportunities for re-teaching a difficult concept, re-phrasing an ambiguous explanation, or re-directing a derailed discussion are created. Examples of these more informal assessments appropriate to the unit level include:

- Monitoring discussions
- Posing questions to specific individuals
- Pop quizzes
- Self assessments
- Quick-writes
- Journal entries

Regardless of whether formal or informal assessment strategies are used at the unit level, linking the assessment to the unit level outcomes is essential.

Comment on On-line Assessments and Grade Books

Many courseware packages include on-line assessment grade book options. Typically, the on-line assessment options only provide for true/false, multiple choice and short answer questions. In some courses, depending on the learner outcome, this is a very appropriate assessment technique and therefore having such an on-line testing option simplifies administering a test. A word of caution, however, regarding on-line testing is necessary. If you plan to give an test on-line, you must make the up front assumption that it is an open book test. Unless you require your students to drive to a proctored testing site, you have no control on the materials the student will have with them when they take the test NOR whether the student who takes the exam is in fact the student enrolled in your course. The proctored testing site is a successful and relatively simple solution to this problem. Perhaps using the on-line testing options as self-assessments for the students as they progress through your course is a more realistic use of this feature.

Another feature of *LearningSpace* and other courseware packages is the Student Portfolio option. The Student Portfolio allows the instructor to maintain an on-line grade book that includes test scores, quiz grades, participation points, project scores, instructor comments, and a variety of other things. In *LearningSpace*, each student is able to access their own Portfolio at any time to keep on-going track of their progress in the course. An example of an Student Portfolio is provided in **Display 3D**.

Display 3D

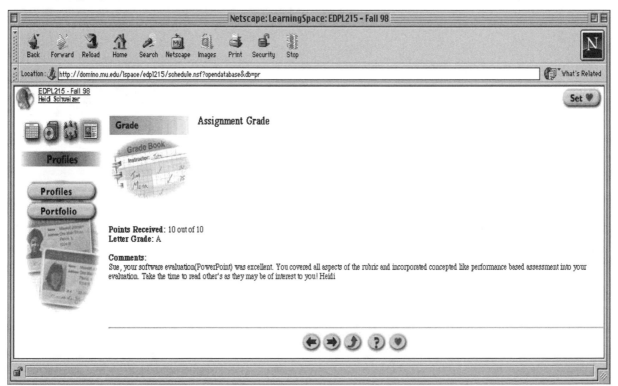

Summary

When you expect your students to demonstrate what they have learned through performance based assessments, you create yet another learning opportunity for students to take the information and skills presented in your on-line course, apply them in thoughtful demonstrations and turn information into meaningful, personal knowledge. Worries about cheating are minimized. But most importantly, no longer are your students just learning about something, they are being and doing something!

It's Your Turn!

Think about a specific student outcome for a course you are teaching or about to teach. List projects that your students could e-mail, fax, or snail mail that would demonstrate their understanding and mastery of the outcome.

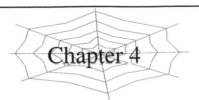

Planning On-line Activities and Resources

Q: What activities are appropriate for on-line learning?

Now the fun begins! Once you have identified your outcomes and aligned your assessments to demonstrations of those outcomes, you are ready to create the activities and resources to support student learning. This is where creating an on-line learning environment that provides fun, freedom, power and belonging becomes so important. This is also where special attention to multiple intelligences and the power of cooperative learning becomes critical.

In Chapter 1, "De-Mystifying the On-line Environment," we discussed in detail the research done by Dr. William Glasser on Control Theory and the four basic psychological needs that drive our behavior: fun, freedom, power and belonging. Dr. Glasser's research demonstrates that if we can create learning environments that satisfy these four basic needs, then learning is optimized. Also, if you recall in that same chapter, we asked you to take a moment and recall a memorable, meaningful learning experience and think about why that experience was such a valuable one. What happened to make it memorable and meaningful to you? This question has been asked of hundreds of students and almost always the answers to this question are related to fun, having choices (freedom), being recognized for knowing (power), feeling challenged (power), and making a personal connection with a teacher, coach or another student (belonging). In addition, these memorable experiences often called upon us to learn in ways that complimented our own unique "intelligences." And, finally, we frequently found students responding to this question with examples of learning that involved some degree of collaboration with others. It becomes our challenge now to recreate these moments in our own on-line courses!

On-line discussions and opportunities to reflect on course readings and personal experiences are an integral part of a quality on-line learning environment. In Chapter 5 of this Guide, considerable attention is given to designing cooperative learning activities and setting up course discussions. In Chapter 6, you will learn how to facilitate and manage those discussions and activities. This section will provide you with an overview of the types of activities that can be used to create and sustain a dynamic on-line classroom that addresses individual learning styles.

Multiple Intelligences and Learning Styles

In 1904, in Paris, French psychologist Alfred Binet developed the first IQ test in response to a need to determine which primary grade students were at risk of failure and

needed remedial help. Binet developed a test that reduced "intelligence" to a single IQ
number that could be objectively measured.

Now, 80 years later, a Harvard psychologist, Howard Gardner, has challenged this
belief. He says that "intelligence refers to the human ability to solve problems or make
something that is valued in one or more cultures."[7]

As further explained by Gardner, IQ is much more than doing well on a "disembodied
language-logic instrument" (i.e. IQ test) in which you are asked to do isolated tasks that you
have never done before and probably will never do again.

Howard Gardner describes eight intelligences and suggests there are many more yet
to be identified. The defining question when asking about intelligences is NOT "how smart
are you, but rather, how are you smart."

- **LINGUISTIC** - (novelist, poet, comedian, newscaster, journalist). The capacity
  to use words effectively–either orally or in writing–story teller, orator, playwright.
  Use language to convince others or to inform others.

- **LOGICAL/MATHEMATICAL** - (accountant, medicine, computer programmer,
  legal, banking, scientist). The ability to use numbers effectively and to be able to
  reason well, be sensitive to cause and effect relationships or if-then relationships.
  Can categorize, classify, calculate, and generalize.

- **SPATIAL** - (architect, interior design, drafting, advertising, painting, sculpting).
  This is the ability to perceive the visual spatial world accurately (hunter–guide);
  or able to transform the environment–such as an interior designer, artist, inventor.
  This is also the ability to visualize and graphically represent ideas and to orient
  one-self in space.

- **BODY-KINESTHETIC** - (athletic, actor, physical education teacher, inventor, or
  dancer). This is the ability to use your body to express ideas–actor, mime, dancer,
  athlete and use your hands to produce or change something such as a surgeon or
  mechanic. Good coordination, balance, dexterity, strength and speed are also
  characteristics of this intelligence.

- **MUSICAL** - (advertising, musician, television personality, composer, music
  teacher sound engineer, film maker). This includes the ability to be sensitive to
  rhythm, pitch, melody.   This intelligence implies an understanding of music from
  an intuitive perspective, from an analytical perspective, or from both.

- **INTERPERSONAL** - (counseling, teacher, politics, religious leader). This is
  the ability to be sensitive to moods, motivations and feelings of other people. It is
  the ability to notice facial expressions, voice, gestures, as well as the ability to
  persuade people to follow you.

- **INTRAPERSONAL** - (psychiatry, guru, philosopher, spiritual leader). This is the ability to have an accurate picture of ones self—one's strengths and limitations. It is a keen awareness of inner moods, desires, motivations, self discipline, self understanding and self esteem.

- **NATURALIST**- (biologist, taxidermist, hunter, conservationist, park ranger, botanist, gardener). The ability to recognize and classify plants, minerals, and animals, including rocks and grass and all variety of flora and fauna.

The research on multiple intelligences suggests that each person possesses all eight intelligences, and that all eight intelligences work together in ways unique to each individual. Most people are highly developed in some intelligences, modestly developed in others and relatively underdeveloped in the rest. An example of one exception to this rule is: Johann Wolfgang Von Goethe - poet, statesman, scientist and philosopher. As David Lazear explains in Seven Ways of Knowing:

> Most people can develop each intelligence to an adequate level of competency if given the appropriate encouragement, enrichment, and instruction. For example, a person with a modest level of musical ability can achieve a sophisticated level of playing the piano given an involved parent, early instruction and exposure to the piano at an early age.

> Intelligences usually work together in complex ways and are always interacting with one another. For example, to play soccer, one needs body intelligence to run, kick and catch, spatial intelligence to orient oneself to the playing field and to anticipate the flying balls, and linguistics and interpersonal skills to successfully argue a point in dispute in the game.

> There are many ways to be intelligent within each category. For example, a person may not be able to read, but can be highly linquistic because he can tell a terrific story or has a large oral vocabulary. Or a person can be a poor soccer player but possess body smarts when she weaves a carpet. People show their intelligences not only within intelligences but between them.[8]

Multiple Intelligences and Technology

Q: How can I use what is known about multiple intelligences to enhance the design of my on-line activities and discussions?

Provide a Variety of Opportunities

When designing on-line learning opportunities, always consider providing a variety of ways students can access information, interact with the information and then demonstrate to you their mastery of the course outcomes. Listed below are the major categories you might want to consider and some suggestions for activities as you begin to create your on-line lessons. Remember, be creative. The ideas are endless!

- **Discussions**: In a cooperative group, share your experiences with using the Internet for research projects in your classroom.

- **Projects**: Create a PowerPoint® presentation to demonstrate an understanding of the conflicts leading up to a war.

- **Interviews**: Invite a children's author for an on-line interview about the emerging reader.

- **Research**: E-mail the Dinosaur Society to find latest research on recent digs in Montana.

- **Critiques**: Develop a list of discussion questions to help students critique particular aspects of an article or video clip to be discussed later in small groups

- **Peer review/reactions**: Have students exchange 'papers' for a peer review. They can use a different font or color to make editing changes.

- **View films/presentations**: Take advantage of streaming video conferencing and put video clips on endangered species in your course.

- **Share and summarize**: Ask a member of each cooperative group to summarize the discussion held in a particular Module.

- **Design Websites, animation, presentations**: Display a gallery of art, science fair project, or invention for viewing and judging by class members or teachers.

To help you see how you can maximize the use of the on-line environment, following are some examples that illustrate the wide range of opportunities for engaging all intelligences through the use of technology:

- Provide print material (textbooks, compilation of readings, or journal articles) for your students. (Verbal/Linguistic)

- Link Web sites to the content. Web sites can provide visual stimulation through colorful images, drawings, diagrams and pictures. (Visual/Spatial)

- Require group work and group discussions. (Interpersonal)

- Use music when appropriate. As an example, one instructor effectively used a video clip explaining copyright law in a "rap" format. (Musical/Rhythmic)

- Use color to distinguish between main topics and sub-topics or to denote instructor versus student comments. (Visual)

- Require students to "reflect" on a journal article. Ask that they relate the important aspects of the article to a personal experience or a personal belief. (Intrapersonal)

- Be "project-based." Request that students create projects to demonstrate their understanding of the major concepts or skills in your course. Learning by doing is an essential part of total learning process. (Body/Kinesthetic)

- Use storytelling to explain a concept. (Linguistic)

- Draw or photograph plants or animals. (Naturalist)

- Write a poem, short play or news article. (Linguistic)

- Make up an analogy to explain an idea. (Logical/Mathematical)

- Record a rap song that explains an event. (Musical)

- Participate in a service project to develop a deeper understanding. (Interpersonal)

- Teach someone in the class something. (Interpersonal)

- Set and accomplish a personal goal. (Intrapersonal)

- Assess your own work. (Intrapersonal)

- Explain your own personal values related to a specific topic. (Intrapersonal)

- Observe, collect and organize data. (Naturalist)
- Draw a conceptual framework for an idea or theory

- Allow final projects to be submitted in a variety of forms -final paper, a PowerPoint® presentation, audio tape, video tape, a multi-media presentation or through video-conferencing; as well as individually or in cooperative groups. (All intelligences)

Take advantage of the wide range of technologies available for teachers and students. Animation, desktop publishing, video-conferencing, presentation software, the Internet, and all forms of multi-media extend the learning environment as far as one's creativity allows. As new technologies are created and imaginations are challenged, the list will grow and so will opportunities for learning to take place in the on-line learning environment.

Displays 4A, 4B, 4C, and 4D are examples of activities from an on-line course *"Foundations of Curriculum."*

Display 4A

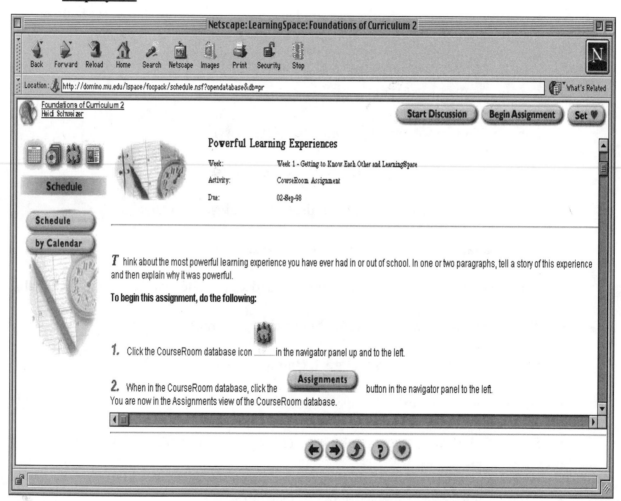

Display 4B

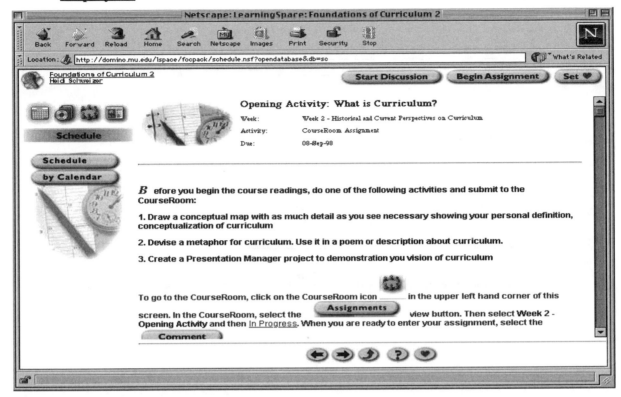

Display 4C

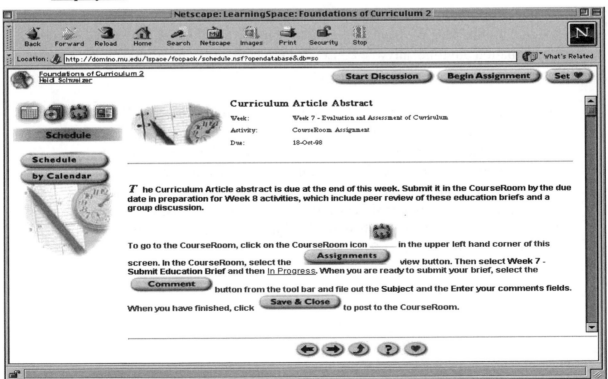

Display 4D

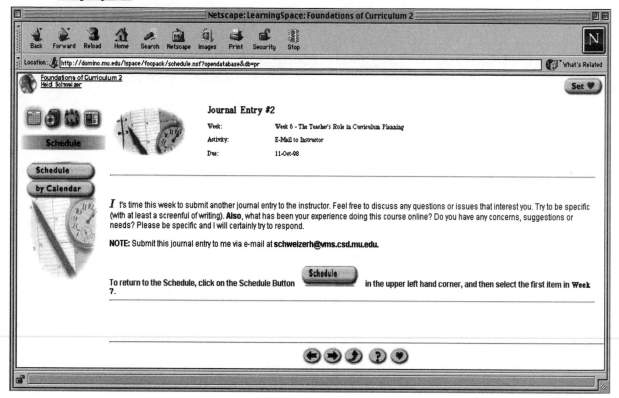

On-line Resources

Resources provide the substance, content and material with which you expect your on-line student to interact. We have the technology today to enable anyone to access virtually any information anytime, anywhere. Lewis Perleman writes in his book entitled School's Out:

> Within the first quarter of the 21st century, information storage will be so compact that all the information a well-informed person could consume in a whole lifetime - all the books, manuals, magazine and newspaper articles, letters, memos, reports, greeting cards, notebooks, diaries, ledgers, bills, pamphlets, brochures, photographs, paintings, movies, TV shows, videos, radio programs, audio records, concerts, lectures, phone calls, whatever - will be able to be stored in an easily portable object, no bigger than a book and potentially as small as a fat fountain pen.[9]

But, as Arthur C. Clarke, science fiction author, so eloquently states:

Before we become too entranced with gorgeous gadgets and mesmerizing video displays, let me remind you that information is not knowledge, knowledge is not wisdom, and wisdom is not foresight. Each grows out of the other and we need them all.

As the developer and teacher of on-line courses, you must take care to provide relevant resources within the context of meaningful activities so as to grow the wisdom and foresight so essential for today's world. Examples of resources that provide a wide variety of opportunities for learners to explore using their own individual talents and preferences include:

- **Articles**: Provide articles in print, rather than electronic form for students to read and reflect on.

- **Website**: Send your students to Websites that provide varying perspectives on a topic.

- **Guest lecturers**: Invite a guest to your 'classroom' who is considered an expert on a specific topic.

- **Textbooks**: Assign chapters in textbooks or other resource books which will enhance your curriculum.

- **Videos**: Use video clips of case studies for students as a source of stimuli for discussion.

- **Lecture notes:** Put your lecture notes on the Web so students can print them out and highlight them for studying.

- **CD ROMs**: Capture video simulations or case studies on CD ROMs for inexpensive and easy dissemination to students in your class.

- **Music**: Use music as a means to teach your students about a particular topic or period in history.

Specific examples of resources taken from the on-line course, *"Foundations of Curriculum,"* are illustrated in Displays **4E, 4F, 4G, 4H, 4I, and 4J**.

Display 4E

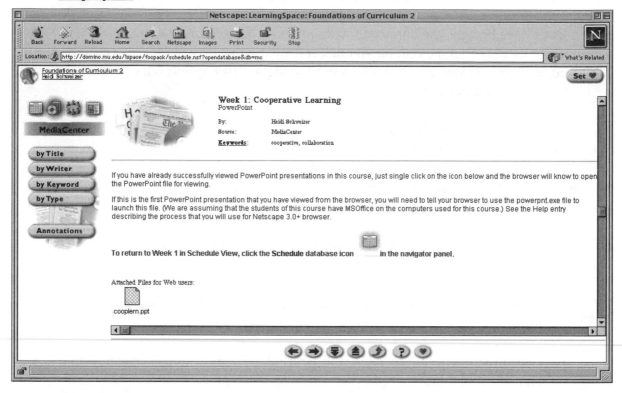

Display 4F

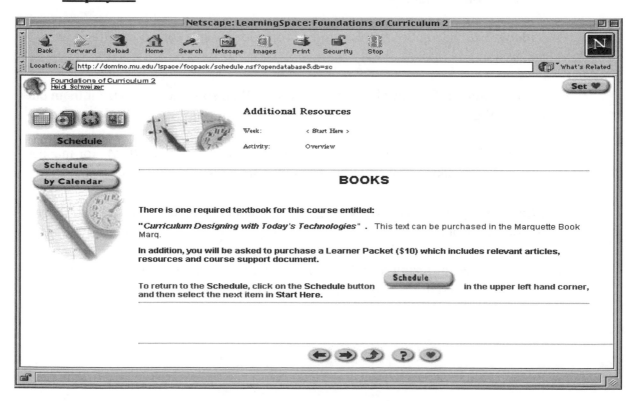

Display 4G

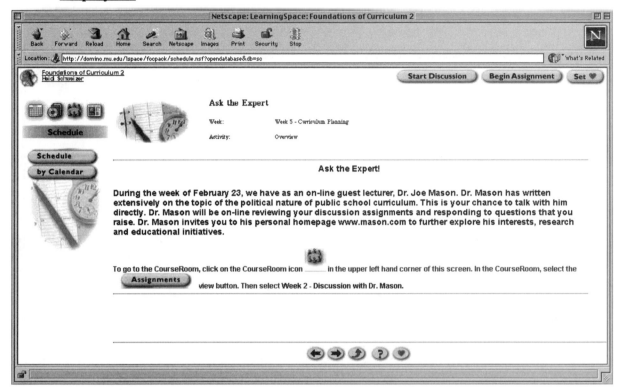

Display 4H

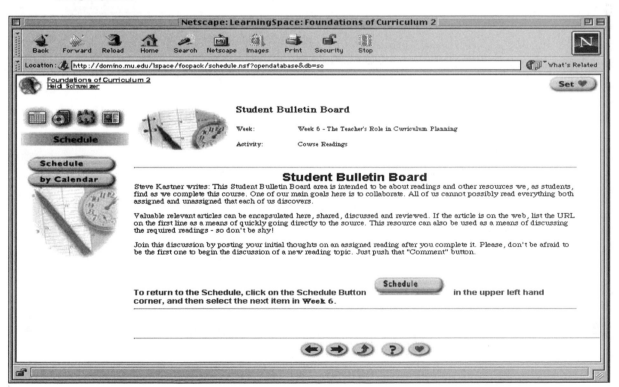

Display 4I

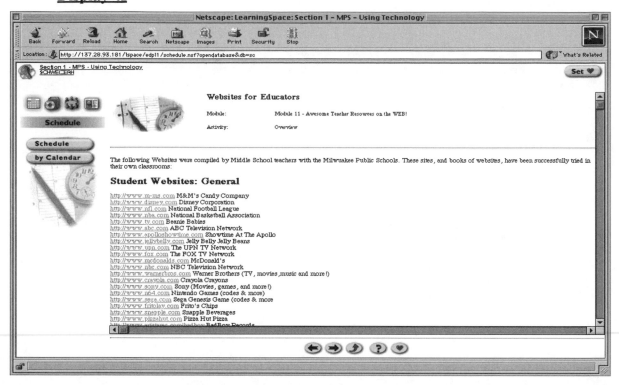

Display 4J

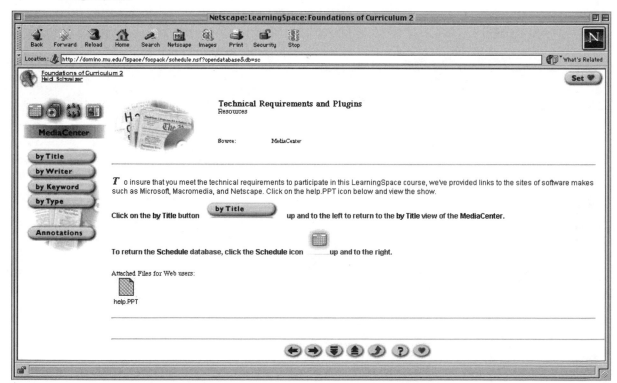

Copyright and Fair Use

Copyright and fair use are not new concepts. From medieval Europe to the present day, those of us who have created, authored or published a work have sought to protect it from being used without our permission. In the United States alone, two hundred years of court rulings demonstrate how controversial copyright and fair use principles can be. And, now as we head full steam into a highly technical world where thc World Wide Web has the potential of providing instant and easy access to just about anything ever created, new and different interpretations of copyright and new and different restrictions on fair use are inevitable.

Copyright is defined as the exclusive right of a creator to reproduce, prepare derivative works, distribute, perform, display, sell, lend or rent their creations.[10] The concept of "fair use" is based in the belief that copying should be allowed for purposes of criticism, news reporting, teaching and scholarly research.[11] For simplicity and clarity, it will be assumed that our discussion here is restricted to **educators who work at non-profit educational institutions**. Copyright and fair use are often at odds: "copyright grants an exclusive monopoly on a particular work; and fair use provides that **someone other than the author** can have certain rights regarding the work ... without payment to the copyright owner".[12]

Before you explore copyright and fair use further, take a look at which types of works a copyright does protect and which types a copyright does not protect.

Copyright protects the following forms of expression and creative works:
√ Poetry
√ Movies and videos
√ A web page
√ Java applets
√ Photographs
√ Artwork
√ Prose
√ Computer programs
√ Music
√ Animations
√ PowerPoint® documents
√ Building plans
√ … and many more

Copyright does NOT protect:
√ Ideas
√ Titles
√ Names
√ Short phrases
√ Facts
√ Logos and slogans (these are protected by trademark)

√   URL'S
√   Works in the public domain (government documents, for example)

The Copyright Act grants five rights to a copyright owner.[13]

1.   The right to reproduce the copyrighted work.
2.   The right to prepare derivative works based upon the original(s).
3.   The right to distribute copies of the work.
4.   The right to perform the work publicly.
5.   The right to display the work publicly.

In addition, the Copyright Act of 1976 set established four provisions by which copyrighted materials could be used in non-profit educational settings. According to author Mary Carter the four "fair use" criteria from the 1976 Copyright Act are:

1.   The purpose and character of the use including whether such use is of a commercial nature or is for non profit educational purposes.
2.   The nature of the copyrighted work
3.   The amount and substantiality of the portion used in relation to the copyrighted work as a whole.
4.   The effect of the use upon the potential market for or value of the copyrighted work.[14]

Copyright and Distance Learning
Q: So what does this all mean for you, the distance educator?

The primary difference between how copyrighted works are protected in the face-to-face classroom and in the distance education cyber-classroom is found in Section 110 of the Copyright Act. In general this section of the law speaks to the types of materials you can realistically expect to use and not be able to use (without permission) in your on-line course. This continues to be a highly controversial area with attempts to negotiate exemptions occurring daily. What follows are the commonly accepted suggestions for what you MAY use in your distance classroom without the permission of the copyright owner:

√   Text
√   A photograph, chart, map or graph
√   A computer screen display, (static - not moving)
√   An illustration
√   A single still frame from a video, videotape, laserdisc. Or from a DVD (Digital Versatile Disc)
√   Portions of audio from non-dramatic music.

Suggestions for what is NOT allowed in the distance classroom (without permission):

√   Full motion video or audio
√   A laserdisc
√   DVD
√   Video file on a computer
√   Consecutive images from a slide set, filmstrip or 16 mm movie
√   Audio from a dramatic work
√   Live performance of a play or musical

The generally accepted rule of thumb is *if it moves, it's not allowed without permission.*

Fair Use Guidelines for Educational Multimedia

In September, 1996, a set of guidelines was developed with the participation of a broad cross section of educators, attorneys, publishers, librarians and other interested parties. These are called the "Fair Use Guidelines for Educational Multimedia."

The commonly accepted definition for "multimedia" is the integration of text, graphics, audio and/or video into a computer-based environment.

The Fair Use Guidelines for Educational Multimedia provide recommendations for specific limits on the amount of copyrighted works that may be used without permission.

√   For motion media–(e.g., video clips) up to 10% or 3 minutes, whichever is less.
√   For text–up to 10% or 1000 words, whichever is less.
√   For poems–up to 250 words. Three poem limit per poet and a five poem limit by different poets from an anthology.
√   For music–up to 10% or 30 seconds, whichever is less.
√   For photos and images–up to 5 works from one author, up to 10% or 15 works, whichever is less, from a collection.
√   Database information–up to 10% or 2,500 fields or cell entries, whichever is less.
√   Also, faculty may retain multimedia products incorporating the copyrighted works of others for a period of two years for educational use. After that, permission must be sought.

The Fair Use Guidelines for Educational Multimedia also provide us the following guidelines:

√   Students may incorporate others' works into their multimedia creations and perform and display them for academic assignments.
√   Faculty may incorporate others' works into their multimedia creations to produce curriculum materials.
√   Faculty may provide for multimedia products using copyrighted works to be

accessible to students at a distance (distance learning), provided that only those students may access the material (password protected courses)
√ Faculty may demonstrate their multimedia creations at professional symposia and retain same in their own portfolios.

While not perfect, the Fair Use Guidelines for Educational Multimedia make it possible for educators and students to proceed with confidence to use small portions of copyrighted works in the creation of multimedia and hypermedia products without permission and without payment to the publisher. The key, as with all practices of fair use, is to use the smallest portion necessary of an educational work to achieve the instructional objective.[15]

Summary

Creating on-line activities and providing on-line resources provides an outlet for your creative juices and playful nature. This is a time to let your imagination run wild as you think of challenging activities and meaningful resources for your students to engage in and explore while at the same time keeping in mind copyright and fair use restrictions.

It is essential to remember that we all learn differently; some of us are much more successful when presented with the written word while others of us excel when asked to explain our ideas in small groups. The activities and resources in your course need to represent a wide range of options for the diverse learners taking your course. The bottom line is: the more we design the core of our instruction around the needs of the LEARNER; the more likely we are to design a course where our students are successful.

On-line In-sites ...

Providing varied activities and encouraging student use of multiple resources in your on-line class will help you create a motivating and inviting learning environment. The following comments from students support this use of creative classroom support.

- *I don't know about you guys, but I really enjoyed the module on e-mail pals. I found out text to be very informative. I particularly appreciated the information presented in the first article we read.*
- *E-mail is a great way of getting people to talk to others they may not otherwise have the opportunity to communicate with.*
- *I just returned from the Website you recommended and I found it to be loaded with information!*

It's Your Turn!

What will you do to create an inviting learning environment for ALL students? Use the following ideas, or create some of your own, to help you design your on-line activities and resources. Take this time to jot down notes in the areas you think you would like to try.

1.   **Link Web sites to the content. (Visual/Spatial)**

2.   **Require group work and group discussions. (Interpersonal)**

3.   **Use music when appropriate. (Musical/Rhythmic)**

4.   **Require students to "reflect" on a journal article. Ask that they relate the important aspects of the article to a personal experience or a personal belief. (Intrapersonal)**

5.   **Be "project-based." Request that students create projects to demonstrate their understanding of the major concepts or skills in your course. (Body/Kinesthetic)**

6.   **Allow final projects to be submitted in a variety of forms -final paper, a PowerPoint® presentation, audio tape, video tape, a multi-media presentation or through video-conferencing; as well as individually or in cooperative groups. (All intelligences)**

7.   **Take advantage of the wide range of technologies available for teachers and students. Animation, desktop publishing, video-conferencing, presentation software, the Internet, and all forms of multi-media extend the learning environment as far as ones creativity allows.**

8.   **Additional ideas**

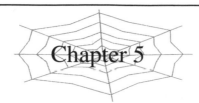

Creating On-line Discussion Groups

Q: How can I set up successful cooperative group interactions in my on-line course?

Whether you are teaching in a traditional face-to-face setting or at a distance with on-line instruction, good teaching and focused learning requires an interactive environment. The research on interactive learning environments is clear and compelling–interactive learning environments have powerful and positive effects on student achievement, self-esteem and the development of higher level thinking skills.

Your challenge will be to create an on-line learning environment that is interactive, collaborative and will help people connect in meaningful, personal ways. Cooperative learning, defined as "instructional use of small groups so that students work together to maximize their own and each other's learning"[16] is one highly effective teaching strategy that ensures a quality interactive environment and easily translates to on-line or web-based instruction.

Grouping Students for On-line Discussions

The first thing you must do is select a course delivery package that makes it easy to set up groups and create opportunities for discussions that are private to a group as well as open to everyone. You must then decide how to group your students. There are three different types of groups you want to consider; keeping in mind that at any given time throughout the duration of your course, all three types of groups could be operating.

Base Groups

A Base Group is a group of students, (usually no more than five) that has as its main purpose to provide each other support, encouragement and assistance needed to successfully complete the course. The group stays together for the duration of the course–beginning and ending the course together. The Base Group is the foundation for a healthy, collaborative environment. When making the decision as to forming a Base Group, consider the following:

- keep the group heterogeneous (gender, ability, ethnic and cultural backgrounds).
- group students together who are geographically close to one another to facilitate off-line interactions.

- give clear and concise roles and responsibilities to each group member. For example, have one member be the **technical support** person (responds to technical questions posed by group members), one member be the **recorder** (enters group decisions for the group into the course, one member be the **facilitator** (ensures that the group is functioning and all members are contributing on-line) and one member be the **checker** to be sure all assignments are handed in on time. (See Appendix 4 for Guidelines for Roles and Responsibilities for Cooperative Group Members.)

Formal Groups

A Formal Group is a group of students who has as its purpose to complete a well defined task–i.e. an assignment, project or presentation. The optimal group size is two or three, but no more than four. The group lasts for the duration of the project, at which time you may want to regroup the students. When making the decision as to who to put into a Formal Group, consider the following:
- have students self-select their groups based on a common interest in a particular topic or assignment.
- group students based on location if location facilitates "off-line" meetings.
- randomly group students.
- give clear and concise roles and responsibilities to each group member to ensure that all members contribute equally and fairly to the group project.

Informal Groups

An Informal Group has as its purpose to focus student attention on selected material to be learned and to ensure that students are thinking (cognitively processing) the information. An Informal Group can provide:
- closure to a lesson ("Choose someone in your Base Group and summarize the discussion in Module 4").
- assurance that misinformation or gaps in instruction are identified ("Choose the person next to you on the class list and describe one key idea you gained from Module 7").
- a quick and easy technique that can be used anytime (the instructor can enter a conversation and pose a quick question just as she might in a face-to-face setting). The optimal group size for an Informal Group is two, but no more than three.

The screen in **Display 5A** provides an example from the on-line course, *"Foundations of Curriculum."*

Creating Cooperative Learning Experiences

Once you have your groups established, both the Formal Groups and the Base Groups, you must consider how to design your instruction so that cooperative learning experiences on-line maximize student learning. David and Roger Johnson, University of

Display 5A

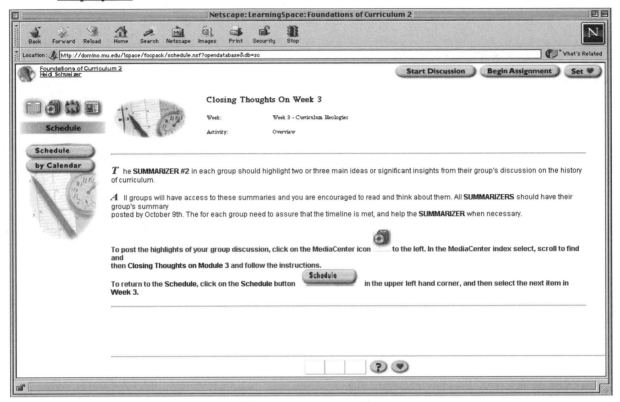

Minnesota, have described five elements that are essential to successful cooperative groups in a face-to-face setting.[17] These elements translate into successful cooperative groups on-line.

Positive Interdependence

Create a "sink-or-swim" attitude! It is essential that you, as an instructor, help create the belief within your groups that "two heads are better than one" and "all or one and one for all." Students must see that they really do need each other to successfully complete the course or a project that is assigned. How is this belief created on-line? Try the following activities:

- **Group Identity** - ask the group members to create a group name. Creative names such as "TNT" (Technology 'n Teaching) "Ladies On-Line" or the "Pioneers" add a bit of fun and creativity to the on-line discussions. (See Appendix 5 for this on-line group activity.) **Display 5B** shows an example of a Group Identity activity as it appears in *LearningSpace*.

- **Which One is False** - a group activity for which each member of the group is asked to come up with three statements about himself (two true and one false), share them with each other on-line and try to figure out which one is false. This serves as a fun way to have students get to know each other and begin to develop a more personal relationship.

Display 5B

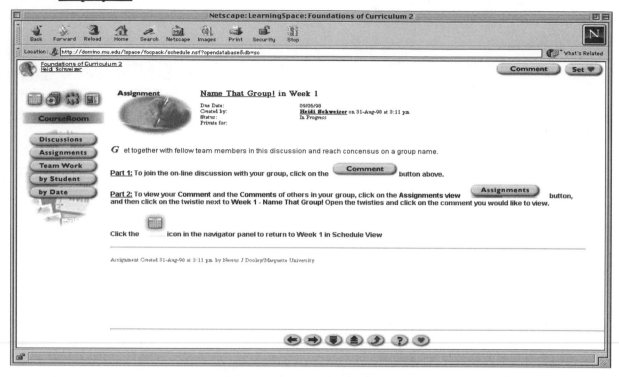

Display 5C shows an example of an "ice-breaker" activity as it appears in *Learning Space*.

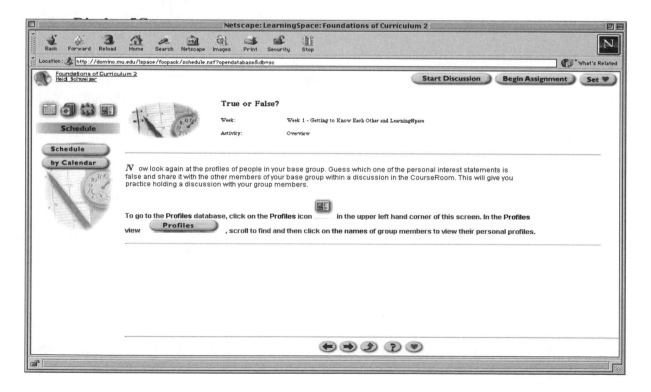

- *Assign Roles and Responsibilities* - **Encourager** e-mails instructor on group cooperation; **Summarizer** writes up group decisions and edits group work. **Checker** is responsible for checking on whether group members understand main concepts. **Technician** is available to other group members for technical advice or assistance. By assigning roles, AND making sure that the student responsibilities are carried out, the group begins to depend on one another to see the value of sharing the load.

Display 5D shows the roles and responsibilities of individual students in an on-line course.

Display 5D

Roles and Responsibilities for Cooperative Group Members

Successful cooperative groups depend on each member taking an active role in assuring the group functions efficiently and effectively with each member "pulling their own weight". There are a variety of ways to help ensure this, one of them en signing specific roles to each member.

Please read the descriptions of the three (3) different roles the members of your group will assume. Discuss them among your group and decide who will do what. Each member must agree to take one responsibility and each role may have up to two people assigned.

Roles

1. **Summarizer** - in some of the Modules the **summarizer** will be asked to summarize the discussion for the week and place it in the MediaCenter for all class members to see.

    _____   _____
    (name)   (name)

2. **Technician** - when fellow group members run into technical problems, the **technician** will be available for extra assistance, encouragement and advice. The **technician** should be the person with the most knowledge about hardware and software questions, problems with the Internet, or quick fixes. The **technician** will also work with the "Technical Assistant" assigned to the class.

    _____   _____
    (name)   (name)

3. **Encourager** - checks on how well the group is functioning. Encourages group members to participate. Informs the instructor of any problems the group is experiencing and helps those that need extra support with a quick e-mail or phone call.

    _____   _____
    (name)   (name)

- *Friendly Competition* - consider setting up competitive situations between groups.

- *Group Reward/Celebration* - recognize good group work, celebrate (a special card by e-mail) the completion of a successful group project.

It is essential that you, as an instructor, frequently assess whether students are pulling their own weight and working together. Ask the group to e-mail you if a problem arises. Ask the observer for regular "progress reports." Continually monitor the on-line discussions for obvious "absences." Call individual group members to determine if they are having difficulties such as connectivity problems, managing an on-line course, or navigating the course.

Individual Accountability

In a successful cooperative group, each member of the group is held accountable for doing his or her own work. Group members know "slackers" are not welcome. It is your responsibility as an instructor to help ensure that everyone contributes their fair share to the group process. How can this be accomplished on-line? Following are some suggestions:

- *Monitor student work.* As an instructor, you must continually review discussion threads, review course work, and check on the progress of assignments.

- *Observer reports.* Expect a group member to report to you on his or her group's project or activity. The observer should poll group members before submitting the report. This responsibility can be rotated among the group members.

- *Randomly "call" on students.* On a random basis, select a student and ask her to explain or comment on a particular aspect of the project.

- *Intervene when a group is struggling.* When it becomes evident in the discussion patterns that a group is having difficulty, intervene, point out the problem, serve as a consultant, but avoid becoming an answer giver. Maintain your role as facilitator.

In **Display 5E** an example which demonstrates the role of the facilitator in an on-line course is shown.

- *Individual assessments.* The best way to ensure individual accountability is to assess each individual student's progress toward mastering the outcomes for the course. Utilize a variety of assessment techniques such as quizzes, papers, reports, projects, or self assessments. If each member of the group realizes that he or she will be held accountable for demonstrating to you a level of mastery of the content, potential slackers become involved students.

- *"Meet" each student on-line (synchronous chat room).* Select a time and ask students to meet with you to assess how they are doing, their progress, and if they have any questions.

Display 5E

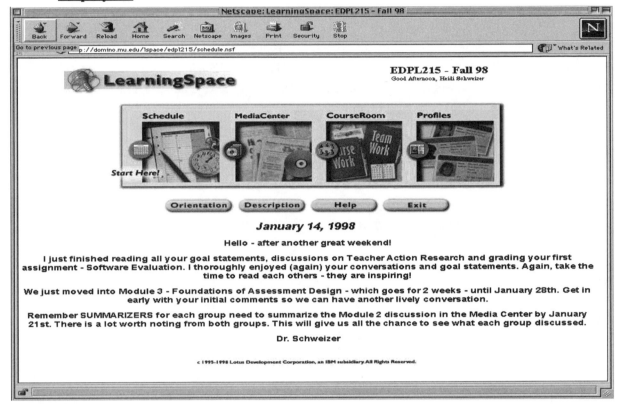

Face-to-Face Interaction

In the traditional classroom, face-to-face interaction would mean sitting "eye-to-eye, knee-to-knee" with other members of the group. The physical proximity is the key ingredient in this element. Without the ability to ask your students to "push your desks together and discuss...," how do you create the sense of proximity on line?

- *Bring the students to the university or workplace.* You may plan to do this a few times throughout the course. This is not always possible, but when it is, it is a powerful way of building group cohesiveness and provides time for students to work shoulder-to-shoulder.
- *Synchronic exercises.* Structure opportunities for students to go on-line together, allowing for immediate feedback and creating a discussion that simulates a "real-life" give and take.
- *Combine the technologies.* When possible, incorporate compressed video, desk-top video or other technologies that allow the students to actually see each other as they discuss a topic or work on a project.

Social Skills

The critical social skills needed for successful group work are:
- get to know and trust each other
- accept and support each other

- communicate clearly
- resolve conflict constructively[18]

As an instructor, you need to actively teach these group skills. A quote from J.D. Rockefeller says it all: *I will pay more for the ability to deal with people than any other ability under the sun.* This means we have to purposefully and precisely teach critical social skills just as we so purposefully and precisely teach the academic skills. Some ideas to build these critical social skills are:

- *Incorporate "scenarios" or case studies into your early modules* that ask students to resolve hypothetical conflicts. For example, ask the students what they would do if one member of their group had not yet posted their response to a question and the success of the group depended on all members posting a response.

Display 5F shows an example of how a "scenario" has been used in an on-line course.

Display 5F

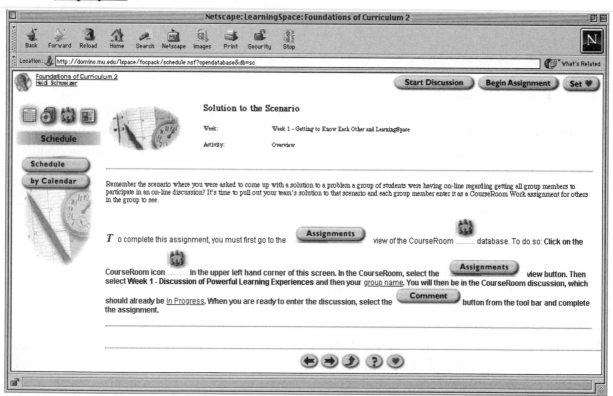

- Give feedback and specific guidance to students when you see they are not communicating as clearly as they could.

Display 5G reveals how an instructor directed the students to specific locations in *LearningSpace*.

Display 5G

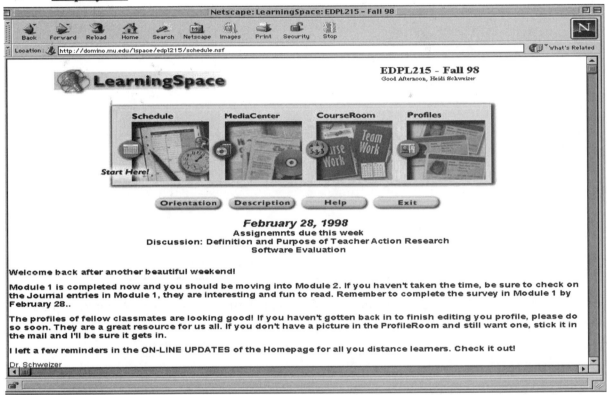

- *Encourage students to discuss topics that might not be related to the course* but that help build acceptance, trust and support of one another.

Display 5H demonstrates the importance of an instructor communicating on a personal level with an individual student.

Group Process

This is simply asking the question "How well did the group achieve its goals and maintain effective working relationships?" As the instructor, you need to continually help students develop and maintain healthy and effective group interaction skills. A good way to do this is to ask your students to reflect on the process of group work. A few ideas to accomplish this include:

- Post processing questions as a final activity in the course. Ask your students to list three things their group did well and one thing upon which they could improve.

Display 5H

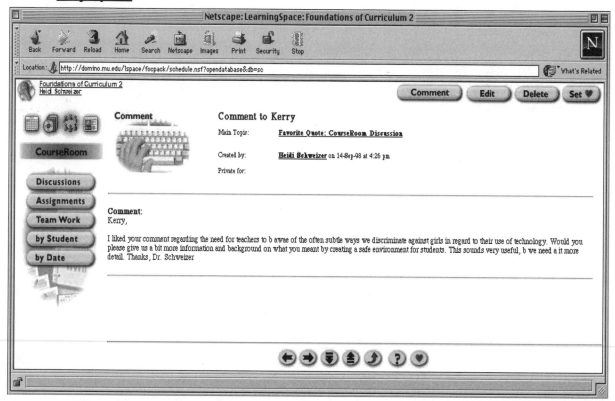

Displays 5I and 5J show examples of students being asked to reflect and comment on the on-line course they have recently completed.

Display 5I

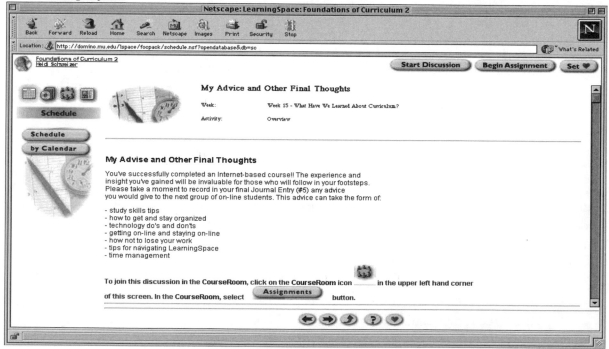

Display 5J

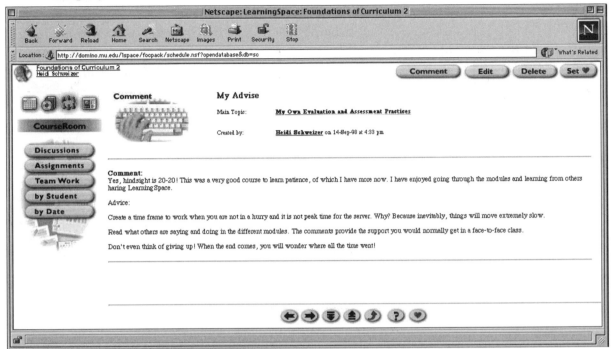

- *Set up a time for a synchronous chat.* Prepare specific questions beforehand so that students will be prepared to give specific examples of what worked and what needed improvement in their group processes.

- *Celebrate!* At the end of the course, provide opportunities for groups to celebrate the hard work and successes they experienced. If it is impossible to schedule a final face-to-face meeting, electronic postcards, fun emoticons, (see **Display 5K**) and a congratulatory note from the instructor to the group are ways to bring positive closure to the group work.

Display 5K

> Emoticons are symbols which instructors and students can use to help them express their emotions which in a face-to-face setting would be referred to "body language." Those invisible emotions, on-line, are now visible through the use of keyboard symbols. Try these out, or make up some of your own!
>
> :)   A smile
> ;)   A wink and a smile
> :-(Sad
> { }   A hug
> :-#   Speechless
> :^)   Just being nosy

Guidelines for Discussions

It is a good idea to establish specific guidelines for your students and provide helpful hints for on-line discussions. The "helpful hints" and guidelines could address topics such as: how often one should go on-line to discuss a particular topic; when to determine if a topic is "done" and it's time to move on; what constitutes a "good contribution;" which emoticons are appropriate or inappropriate; time frames for discussion; and being consider-ate and sensitive to others. **Display 5L** shows a sample of Discussion Guidelines.

Display 5L

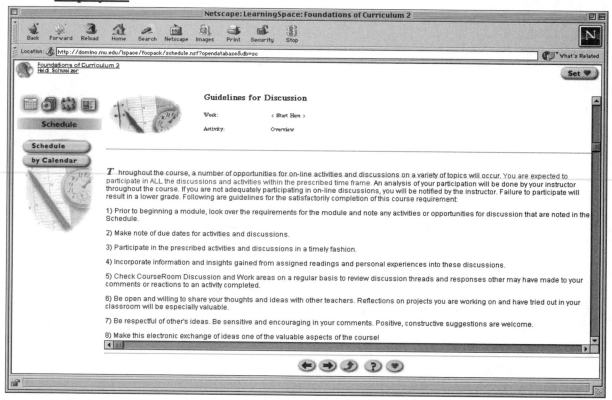

Summary

Creating interactive learning environments are essential if you expect your students take the information that you provide and turn it into meaningful "knowledge". Larsen (cited in Fox, 1991) states that the confusion between knowledge and information:

is perhaps one of the most serious and widespread mistakes in the current use of information technology, and it leads to the attitude that giving students information is identical to giving them knowledge.[19]

According to Judi Harris, "knowledge is a result of the process of knowing, which can only occur as the learner actively constructs what he or she knows, using information in this process."[20] Creating interactive learning environments where students take the information and "play with it"–apply it to their personal lives, expand it to explain a personal experience, or change it to create a new personal perspective are essential to ensure learning takes place.

On-line In-sites ...

Whether taking a course in a traditional face-to-face setting or at a distance with on-line instruction, good teaching and learning require an interactive and collaborative environment. The following student comments reveal the importance of collaboration, sharing of ideas, and creating a supportive, caring climate for learning.

- *Communicate, on a regular basis, with one or more people from the class so that you know what you're doing. This will help to keep up your morale.*
- *Take seriously the roles of your group members and use your group to get advice and encouragement.*
- *Don't be afraid to ask for help!*
- *Work in partners. It really lessons the workload. Divide up some of the assignments between you.*
- *When working in cooperative groups, if one person doesn't know the answer to a question, you can always call the instructor or another student. This is a wonderful learning process!*

 It's Your Turn!

1. **Describe an activity/lesson for which students will be required to work in groups during your course. How will you group students? What should students expect to gain from working in the group setting?**

2. **Plan an activity that will reinforce the social skill "know and trust each other."**

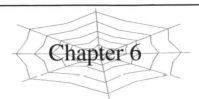

Chapter 6

Being a "Visible" On-line Instructor

Q: What does it take to successfully facilitate learning on-line?

Just as the successful classroom teacher acts as a facilitator, monitor, guide, lecturer, consultant, counselor, moderator and manager, so goes the successful on-line instructor. The skills needed to guide a student through a successful learning experience are just as varied and important for on-line instruction (if not more so), as they are for face-to-face instruction. An instructor skilled in both managing and facilitating is paramount when it comes to maintaining interactive, thoughtful, creative, and fun learning environments that students look forward to joining.

As a facilitator, you will be responsible for creating and organizing the course activities and discussions. It will be up to you to make sure that students are actively participating in the class. It will also be important for you to be "visible." That is to say, you will need to be on-line to ask questions as well as moderate and summarize discussions; or ask students to summarize. As a manager, you will also be responsible for enforcing rules and guidelines and making sure that everyone adheres to those guidelines. Off-line you will be keeping records and preparing for discussions which will take place with your students.

Your Role as a Facilitator

The challenge of teaching on-line rests with the teacher's ability to clearly communicate expectations, personalize the learning environment and inspire thoughtful discussions.

Communicate

It is essential to have clearly written directions and instructions for all aspects of the course that are easy to find and easy to follow. For example, clearly established learner outcomes for the course become the foundation for providing your on-line students with a clear road map of where you are going and what can be expected. Unambiguous directions for projects or discussion assignments, assessments with well-defined rubrics, and complete instructions for navigating the course need to be communicated to all students in a well-written, printed document (Learner Packet) as well as posted in an easily accessible spot on-line. When developing your on-line course, try out your instructions and directions in a "pilot" project to determine where changes and refinements are needed.

Display 6A shows an example of an on-line assignment. Note the organization and clarity of instruction.

Display 6A

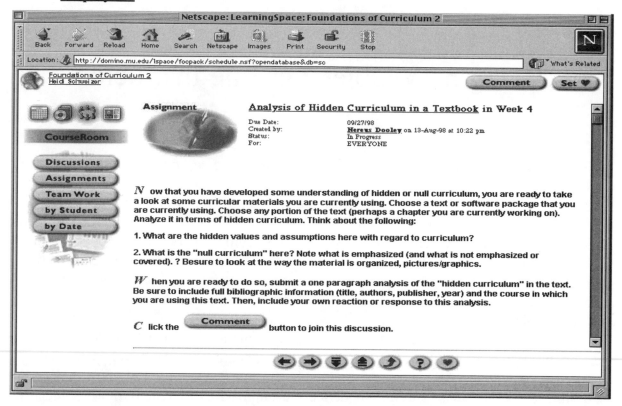

Personalize the Learning Environment

Students on-line need to know that someone is "out there" who cares about their success. In a face-to-face classroom, a wink, smile, spontaneous word of encouragement or "How was your week-end?" goes a long way in making personal connections with your students. How can you establish an environment of genuine care on-line?

- Ask students how they would like to be addressed. When appropriate, use first names when responding to students' comments or work assignments. This personal touch instantaneously creates a sense of "She's talking to ME!"

Displays 6B and 6C show how students can be encouraged and challenged to participate on-line in a friendly, inviting tone.

- Be responsive to concerns and questions raised. Address concerns and questions within a timely fashion; always following the office hours you have set up with your students in the beginning of the course. For example, if you tell your students that you will be on-line everyday from 3:00 - 6:00 p.m. to respond to any comments or questions in the course, then BE THERE!   If you tell your students you will be checking the course everyday, Monday through Friday, twice a day, then do it. How you manage the time you spend "in the course" is up to you.

Display 6B

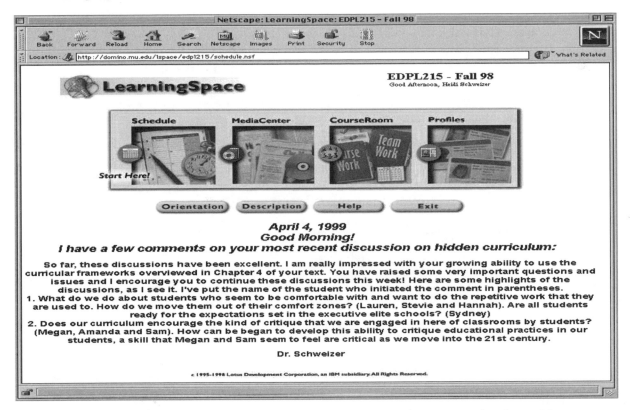

However, the more accessible and timely you are in communicating with your students, the more your students will feel committed to successfully completing your course.

- Have a sense of humor. On-line instruction AND learning can, at times, be frustrating given the ever changing nature of technology. We often think that technology is perfect and therefore do not expect browsers to crash, servers to go down or software to falter. A good sense of humor can go a long way in a some-times frustrating environment.

- Use an informal but clear writing style. Be complete in your responses. Comment as if you were writing a friendly letter. Remember, your students cannot "see" your non-verbal cues, and as a result are much freer to read into your comments whatever they might imagine. A friendly, complete and encouraging response is most often well received and enhances the learning process.

- Comment to individual students on events outside of the class that may be of personal interest to them. Be aware that these exchanges should not take up a lot of space in the course; but a sentence or two on "How was your Thanksgiving?" or "What did you think of those Packers?" creates another important personal connection.

Display 6C

Display 6D shows an example of a Thank You note written to an on-line student by instructor.

The Discussion Leader-Discussion Creator

You are the person who guides, directs, and redirects the discussion. It is a critical role in on-line instruction and requires thoughtful attention to detail.

- Be mentally prepared. When you go on-line to facilitate a discussion, be as prepared as you would be when you step in front of 50 students in your face-to-face class. Give your students the time, attention, and focus they deserve. If your mind is on other things, the quality of your responses will suffer. Set aside a specific amount of time that allows you to thoughtfully read and respond to your students.

- Be accurate. You are often the content expert and responsible for "good" information. If you don't know the answer to a question, say so and then go find it. Be sure to follow up on all promises that "I'll get back to you with that information."

- Clarify any misunderstandings or ask members of the group to help each other clarify their thoughts. Monitor the discussions closely so that misunderstandings or "gaps" in understanding are detected early.

Display 6D

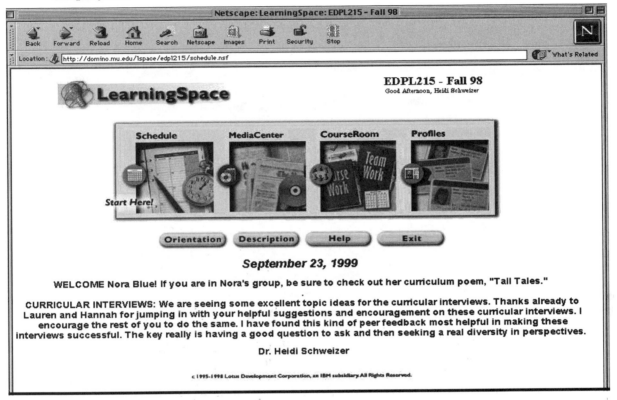

- Refer students to comments made by other students in the class. One of the major advantages of on-line courses is that all discussions and work assignments are recorded and can be easily recalled, referred to or even indexed for future use. Take advantage of this wonderful resource of ideas, opinions and thoughts.

- Summarize discussions when appropriate. Depending on the size of the group, it is possible that a discussion could take up many, many screens, thus becoming "too much" to use effectively. An excellent way to bring closure to a unit before going to the next unit is to ask a member of a discussion group to summarize the discussion for the rest of the group. This summary now becomes the resource for students to refer to and the expanded discussion is archived. The instructor can also provide a summary along with comments to bring the unit to conclusion.

- Error on the side of becoming involved in a group discussion too much rather than too little. Students want to know you are out there; listening, reflecting on what they have said, and interested in their thoughts. Be visible and a frequent contributor to the conversation.

- Raise questions and check for answers. A good facilitator asks more questions than gives answers. Inspire reflective thought. Push for deeper understanding. Do not accept superficial answers. Insist on complete and thoughtful contributions.

Note in **Display 6E** how the instructor monitored the group discussion between students.

Display 6E

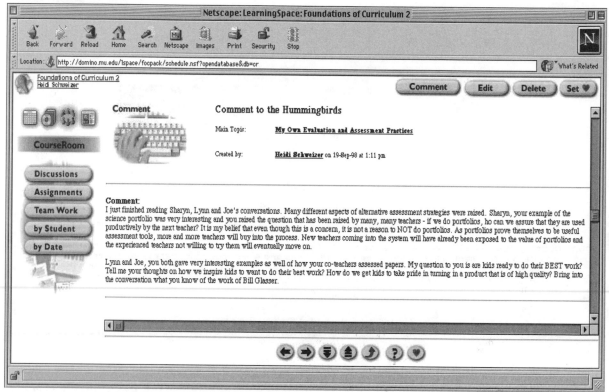

Display 6F is an example showing how the facilitator guides and encourages students through good questioning.

- Ensure that all students are respectful and responsible in their responses and interactions with other members of the class. Establish clear guidelines in the beginning and follow through. A telephone call or e-mail to an errant student may be necessary.

Your Role as a Manager

Q: How do I manage an on-line environment so that my students will have a well–coordinated, organized experience?

Managing your on-line course so that students feel empowered to take charge of their own learning presents its own special challenges. How do you manage a course so as to maintain cohesiveness but not over manage so as to stifle discovery learning? Key components of a well managed course are: establish a record keeping system, set and maintain timelines, and enforce rules and guidelines.

Display 6F

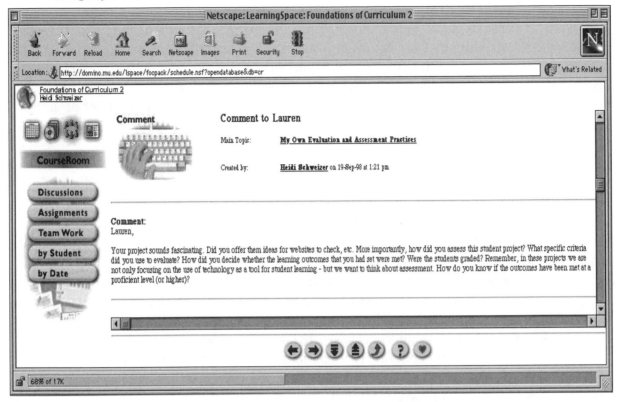

Establish a Record Keeping System

Depending on the number of students taking your on-line course, record keeping can become as important to good instruction as your facilitation skills! A good interactive and project-based course implies students are on-line discussing, sharing ideas, posting projects and reflecting on their experiences. How do you, as an instructor, keep track of all this data?

The key to managing large amounts of data is to create a manageable and easy to use record keeping system. A "grid" that lists the students on the left (by cooperative groups) and each required discussion or project (by module) across the top provides a simple and very handy way of recording data (Appendix 6). When a student's comment or contribution to a discussion is read, the instructor records either a plus, check or minus next to the student's name. A plus indicates the comment was well done and complete, a check indicates a satisfactory comment and a minus an unsatisfactory comment. A quick glance at the grid at any time during the course gives the instructor a summary of who is participating and at what level. The grid can then be used to support a grade given at the end of the course.

If possible, engage a graduate student or office assistant to regularly check on the progress of all students in the class. Such a person would simply check which students have been on-line and contributing. It is not necessary that the assistant read or evaluate the comments; only to tally who has successfully and in a timely fashion completed required assignments and discussions.

Set and Maintain Timelines

One of the key obstacles for the student to overcome when taking a course on-line is the enormous temptation to "put off" completing assignments. Since the student is no longer accountable for showing up for class every Monday and Wednesday from 2:00 to 3:30 p.m., it becomes very easy to fall into the "out of sight, out of mind" way of thinking. You, as an instructor, can provide the necessary structure to address this problem.

There are a variety of ways to structure a course in terms of when modules or units should be completed and projects, discussions, and assignments need to be "turned in." One highly successful format is to assign a block of time to each unit or module in the course (i.e. Module 1 will take place the week of Sept. 7th and end Sept 14th). By doing this, you are assuring that when a specific topic is to be discussed, all students will be involved and discussing that topic. This format frees students from having to go back and check the discussion areas of modules they have completed and provides them with clear guidelines for assignment due dates. They will know that during a specific time period they are responsible for reading and participating in an on-line discussion.

Just as there are timelines to complete a module and participate in the on-line discussion, so are there timelines or due dates for projects. These dates should be clearly posted (preferably in both the print material you distribute as well as conveniently located on-line.) Have a policy for accepting (or not accepting) late assignments.

Students who are not adhering to timelines need to be contacted immediately. The instructor needs to determine why the timelines have not been met (i.e. technical problems) and a consistent and fair solution needs to be implemented.

The distance learning equivalent to "the dog ate my homework" is "the dog chewed my cable connection," "the server was down" or "I worked five hours, got ready to save and close and my work disappeared." The fair and caring instructor has always listened to reasons why his or her student was late with an assignment and then made a judicious decision as to consequences. In the on-line environment the scope of potential "excuses" becomes much broader and more difficult to control. All the connectivity related issues, in addition to hardware and software problems, create enticing opportunities for the errant student to squeeze out a little extra time to turn in an assignment. Following are a few suggestions to help the student stay on track:

- Suggest that students ALWAYS complete their assignments off-line and save them on a disk. When they are ready, they can then go on-line and either copy and paste or attach the document for posting in the course. This eliminates assignments lost in cyberspace and subsequent frustrated students.

- Let your students know of ways that they may be inadvertently "kicked off line," thus losing anything they may have been working on. For example, if their teenage son picks up the extension, or they have not disabled 'call waiting,' the connection to their on-line service will terminate.

- Set clear expectations regarding deadlines for work assignments and discussions and the consequences if they are not met. Include these guidelines both on-line and in printed form. During the first week of class, draw attention to your expectations and give your students the opportunity to clarify any misunderstandings. Then stick to them!

- Set up alternatives for submission of assignments and communicating with you in case you really do experience a major technical breakdown. Create an address list of all students in the course so you can e-mail them if the server on which your course resides goes down. Compile a list of fax numbers for students in case the e-mail system is also inoperable. A phone tree, put together in the first week of class, gets a message out to a large number of students quickly. Whatever your plan, it needs to be in place early. (See Appendix 1 for an example of Emergency Guidelines.)

Enforce Rules and Guidelines

As the instructor for an on-line course, it is important that the guidelines and rules you set in the beginning of the course and clearly noted in course print material are consistently followed. A few tips to maintain an orderly on-line environment include:

- Monitor on-line behavior and if a problem arises, address it immediately. Remember, there is a tendency to "say" things on-line that should not be "said" if standing face-to-face.

- Return projects and take part in discussions in a timely fashion. If you expect students to submit assignments on time, set a good example.

- Adhere to fair use and copyright laws and expect your students to do the same.

- Keep clear and concise records for easy reference and accurate data.

Display 6G shows an example of how the instructor stepped in to maintain an orderly classroom.

Keep Your "Cyber Classroom" Picked-Up and Orderly

When teaching a web-based course, your classroom becomes the discussion and work areas of the groupware product you are using. And, as your course progresses, you will notice that the student discussion and work areas will become quite busy and very full. The students' thoughts, ideas, questions, comments, stories and examples are all rich sources of information upon which all students in the class can draw. However, just as you would not allow students to jump randomly from one topic to another in the face-to-face classroom, with no common thread to pull the ideas together, neither do you want your course discussion and work area to appear disconnected or disorganized. All the careful pre-planning in the world on your part will not prevent some students from entering comments in the course

Display 6G

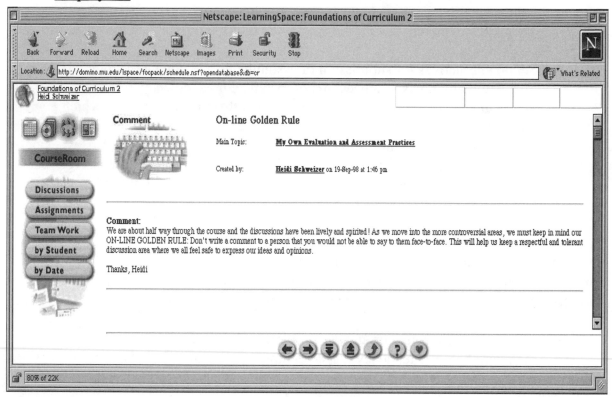

discussion or work area in an incorrect place. When this occurs, the course room discussion area appears to be very confusing for the other on-line students. It will be your responsibility, as the manager for your course, to move comments (either cut and paste or use the tools within the program) to assure that the flow of conversation is natural and easy to follow.

Summary

Independent, self-directed learning is the name of the on-line learning game. And, when taken seriously and confidently, the on-line learner extends his own learning far beyond traditional learner in the traditional classroom. Unfortunately, not everyone has the self-discipline nor past opportunities to "practice" taking charge of one's own learning. It now becomes important that you, the instructor, design an environment that is structured (timelines, deadlines and logical consequences if timelines are not met). This structure will provide the guideposts for a learning journey that will take each student in a different direction, but ultimately end up all in the same place. Providing structure in your course will help reduce the problems you will have as an instructor with students who have not yet mastered the skill of self-directed learning.

The art of on-line teaching requires a wide variety of skills including organization, communication and human relations. Care for the individual becomes the norm as you the instructor individualize your comments to meet the special needs of each of your students. On-line teaching is a personally satisfying, frequently challenging and a very powerful means to enhance learning and ensure student success.

On-line In-sites ...

The distance learning equivalent to "the dog ate my homework" is "the server was down" or "the dog chewed the cable." In an on-line environment, the scope of potential "excuses" for not completing assignments on time becomes much broader. This section provides advice for the on-line student on how to get and stay organized, as well as how to maximize the on-line experience.

- *Get on-line every day, if possible. You need to read the assignments, comments, and other information and then log off to formulate your own responses. Then you log on again to enter your information. It takes a day or more to get feedback on what you submitted, and then you need to respond back to the feedback.*
- *Keep up with the assignments!*
- *Copy the names of classmates and projects that are interesting, establish networks/contacts for future use.*
- *Set aside the same time every week to go on-line. Allow at least four hours of time and don't miss a week. Be sure it is away from kids, spouses, homework, etc. The work cannot be done quickly, and it's important to take the time to read the other students' comments and to go back and read the instructor's comments on previous modules. I really found out too late the value of reading the statements of others.*

 ### It's Your Turn!

As an on-line instructor, you will encounter situations which you will need to handle, both off-line and on-line. Use the following hypothetical situations as an opportunity for you to practice and prepare yourself for the 'real moment' when you will need to address a concern. **What would you do if...**

1.   **You have a student who does not log on. (This happens ALL the time!)**

2.   **One of your students is entering other groups conversations and you are getting complaints from these students.**

3.   **You have a student who has not yet mastered the skill of where to 'nest his comments.'**

4.   **One of your students is constantly complaining on-line.**

5.   **A student in one of the groups is disrespectful of others ideas.**

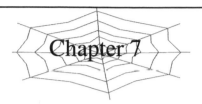

Technology

Q: How can I help make the technology transparent for the on-line learner? Do on-line learners need to be technically savy to be successful?

For the first time on-line learner, your major concern for the first two or three weeks of your on-line course will be related in some way to software or hardware troubleshooting. Your students are entering a new learning environment, totally dependent on the availability of working technology. Some of the problems may be out of your control (i.e. the students cannot access their on-line service or the university server, upon which your course resides, because it has decided not to respond). In other incidences, you may find that you will be able to help your students (i.e. configuring their laptop, or downloading programs). Whatever the case may be, you need to be prepared to help your students overcome technology related problems or refer them to a person who can!

Server Administrator

It is important to remember that you are the instructor, not the technician. A successful teaching and learning experience for all involved in an on-line course is dependent on a knowledgeable, friendly, and helpful technician who is familiar with the server on which your course resides and the software by which your course is delivered. This person, usually designated as the Server Administrator, needs to be readily available for consultation in both the course development phase as well as when you are teaching the course.

An alternative to building and teaching your course on an "in-house" server with your own resident technician is to out-source this service. Instead of building a network to handle your courses and hiring the staff to manage, support and maintain it (upgrades, storage, backups, security, and so on) you could choose a commercial provider as a solution. When deciding which commercial provider to use, consider the following:

- Experience. How long has the company provided network-based hosting using your particular software requirements?

- Cost. Can you select precisely which parts you would like hosted? Does the provider offer usage-based pricing that ensures that you pay only for what you use?

- Time. How soon can they get you up and running?

- Reliability and Security. Can you trust the provider with your data?

- Global Accessibility. Will your course be offered around the globe? If so, does the provider have the appropriate access points?

- Customer Support. Does the provider ensure helpdesk support and technical assistance in a timely fashion?

Regardless of your decision to either outsource the hosting of your course, or purchase the hardware and support personnel to maintain your own system, it is essential that complimentary and competent technical support is readily available to you as you design and teach your course.

Minimum Hardware Requirements

On-line course environments can require a wide range of acceptable hardware in order to operate efficiently and effectively. Whatever the hardware requirements for your course, be sure to clearly communicate them to your students. Include in this checklist:

√   appropriate platform–platform refers to general types of computers, in most cases, either IBM compatible (PC) or Macintosh. It must be made clear with which platform your computer is compatible.

√   hard disk space–refers to the amount of memory needed to efficiently run the programs necessary for your course. This is usually stated in RAM (random-access memory) and will vary widely depending on the types of applications you have built into your course.

√   monitor requirements–refers to the video screen or sometimes called CRT (cathode-ray tube). Requirements to consider are: color, graphics support, and size of screen.

√   modem speed–refers to the device that connects your computer to a telephone line or some other conduit for sending and receiving data. Modems are built for different levels of speed and efficiency. Faster modems transmit signals quickly and diminish the time needed to load a screen or browse the Internet. Realistically, set minimum limits on the modem speed required for your course.

√   soundcard–a soundcard enables the student to hear voices, music and other sound bytes through their computer. If you enable audio applications in your course, be clear that your students will need a soundcard in order to access them.

√ connections to the Internet–once you have a computer, a modem, and the appropriate software, you need to have some way to connect your computer to other computers. There are commercial ventures that provide Internet access (AOL, EXECPC. PRODIGY, COMPUSERVE, etc.) In addition, many school districts and universities provide free Internet access through their networks.

√ recommended browsers–a browser is the software needed to access the Web. Netscape and Internet Explorer are two examples of the most popular browsers.

√ websites for downloading browsers–whenever possible, provide accurate websites for quick and easy downloading of the appropriate browser.

(See Appendix 7 for a sample technology requirements checklist.)

Display 7A gives a sample of the recommended hardware and software from the course, *"Foundations of Curriculum."*

<u>Display 7A</u>

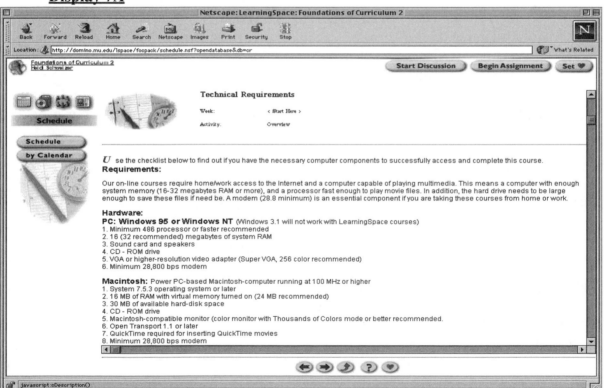

Be Prepared to Handle Problems

Most likely a number of your students will experience problems with their personal computers or laptops. Configuring access to their on-line service, downloading a browser, or launching a program can present frustrating and time-consuming obstacles for the user. A few suggestions for addressing this problem are:

- Provide access to a technical consultant (either face-to-face or an 800 number) for a specific time period. For example, every Saturday from 9:00 - 12:00 a technician could be available on campus for students willing and able to drive to campus.

- Provide technical help on-line within the course. Students experiencing a particular problem can describe the problem on-line and a technician is contracted to respond within 24 hours. The problems and responses can be indexed and organized into a very useful on line data base for students to trouble shoot their own problems.

- Use the expertise of other members in the course. As students in the course encounter and resolve various technical problems, have a designated location in the course where the problem and resolution can be posted along with a telephone number of a willing helper.

Display 7B is an example of the On-line Technical Support used in the course entitled, *"Foundations of Curriculum."*

Display 7B

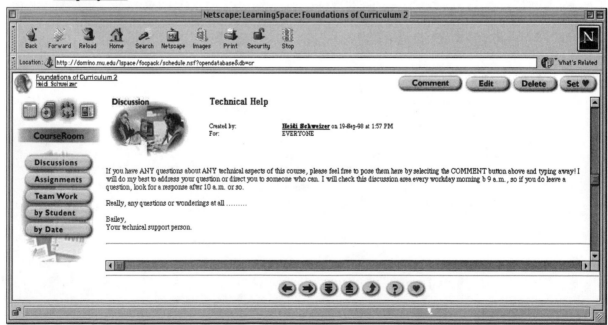

Display **7C** and **7D** are examples of the Emergency Guidelines and Emergency Instructions for students in the on-line course, *"Foundations of Curriculum."*

Display 7C

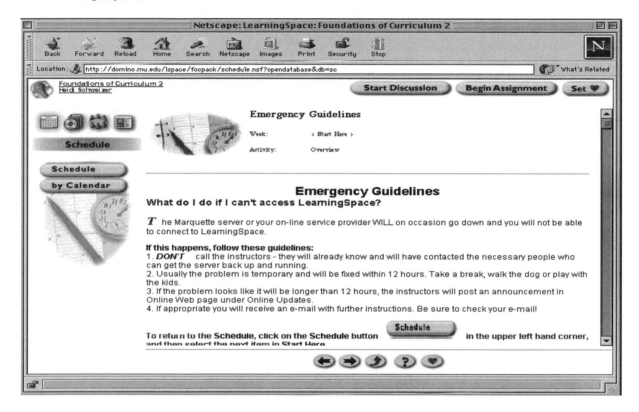

Display 7D

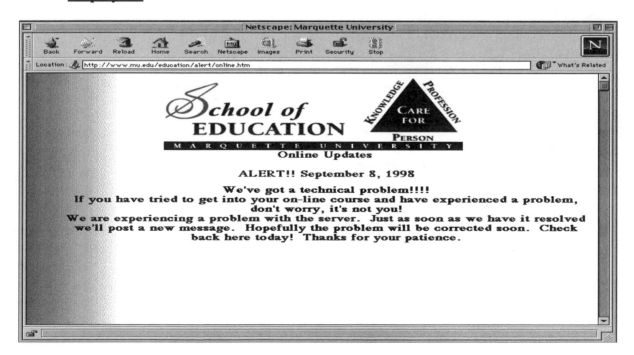

Student Support

In addition to recommendations for providing the on-line student with technical support, students need support in other areas of the on-line learning environment. For example, questions relating to specific course content, course expectations, testing proce-dures, availability of course textbooks and resources, how to add or drop a course, or what the availability is for future on-line courses. Just as you need to provide student support for technical questions, so is support needed for the common questions that come up when students are taking a course at a distance. They are not able to just drop into the front office to get an answer. Options for additional student support include:

- An 800 number with qualified personnel to answer academic questions.

- An on-line help area where questions can be answered quickly and completely. As in the on-line technical help, this can become a quick reference area of FAQ (frequently asked questions).

- Anticipate the questions that are most apt to come up and provide answers and information in a student handout to be distributed in the beginning of the course. This "handout" can also be given out electronically.

- Provide specific e-mail addresses and phone numbers for the bookstore, academic services, admissions, school office and instructor's office. Be sure to include the hours these various people can be reached.

Summary

As an instructor, you need to determine the level of technical sophistication and distance learning experience of the students taking your on-line course. You may not require any previous computer experience or you may require that your on-line students have previ-ous experience with specific software packages and browsers prior to taking your course. If your students have no previous distance learning experience, you may want to consider additional support up front to make the transition a successful and seamless one. Whatever your decision, be prepared to provide the level of technical assistance and academic counsel-ing necessary to support student learning.

On-line In-sites ...

Students are entering a new learning environment, totally dependent on the availability of working technology. A major concern of on-line students, primarily in the first few weeks of a course, has to do with, in some way, software or hardware problems. Following are student reflections on what works and what doesn't work on the technology front.

- *Great Grampa Werner always used to say, "Only a poor workman blames his tools." My advice is to persevere through the technical difficulties (admittedly fewer by the end of the course) in order to experience the benefits of what your classmates are thinking and doing with the coursework.*
- *Make sure you know how to e-mail!*
- *Eat your dinner while you wait between commands.*
- *Make sure your computer is working right in the first class. Mine had two major problems and cost me time that I could not afford.*
- *Work during the Packer game-it's a lot easier to get on-line and stay there because no one else wants to work then. (You can always have the game on TV while you work.)*
- *Watch the phone jack, especially if you have a wall mounted phone. The plastic piece does break when forced too often.*
- *Create a time frame to work when you are not in a hurry and it is not peak time for the server. Why? Because inevitably, things will move extremely slow.*
- *Try to remember that technology makes your life easier.*

 It's Your Turn!

How will you provide technical help for your students? Take this opportunity to write your Emergency Guidelines for On-line assistance. If you are unclear or untrained in this area, it will be helpful to find a technology expert at your location who can help you get started.

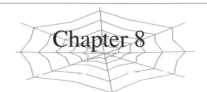

Chapter 8

The Final Two Spins:
Evaluation and Visual Design

Q: How important is the visual appeal of my course? What is a good on-line course evaluation?

By now, you should be ready to take your web-based course on-line. You have created a course that incorporates the eight multiple intelligences, Control Theory, and performance assessment. Your course is learner centered, containing interesting and highly interactive activities. The resources you have identified for your students support your course outcomes and provide current, insightful and interesting content. A student support system is in place to answer both technical and procedural questions. You are ready to teach! Before you begin, however, consider two additional areas to address: course evaluation and visual design.

Designing a Course Evaluation

A course evaluation is an instrument designed to give you, the instructor, feedback on how well your accomplished the following:

- Enabled your students to meet the stated course outcomes

- Created a viable and rich learning environment

- Provided for quality instructor feedback, interaction and facilitation

- Included relevant and meaningful resources and activities

- Resulted in a rich, successful learning experience

Display 8A is an example of a course evaluation shown in *LearningSpace*.

Display 8A

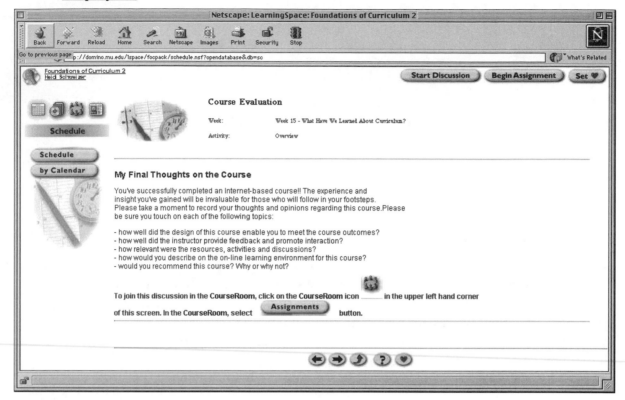

Evaluation Formats

Course evaluations come in many different formats. Most higher education institutions require students to complete a standard course evaluation form. The results of these are centrally tabulated and shared with the instructor. Some instructors choose to develop their own, more specific course evaluations that they administer, in addition to the standard one. Other institutions or organizations have nothing in place for course evaluation and, in fact, overlook the invaluable information and insights that can be gained from administering one. Whatever your situation, a course evaluation is an extremely important component of the development and delivery of your on-line course.

An example of a course evaluation, designed by instructors looking for very specific feedback, is provided in Appendix 8 of this book. In general, from a course evaluation you will learn:

- What students liked and didn't like

- Parts of the course you may remove next time

- Segments of the course that need additional resources or activities

- How to better facilitate on-line student learning

- Things you will never do again

- Impressions of the students' on-line experiences

- How you could structure the course differently to ensure that all students are successful

Your on-line evaluation will be extremely helpful in further planning of your course. Revising and updating course materials and activities are necessary for any course, whether delivered on-line or face-to-face. Course evaluations provide you with meaningful information upon which future changes in your course can be based.

As you develop and then administer your course evaluation, keep the following key ideas in mind:

1. Consider keeping the evaluation confidential to increase the quality of the responses.
2. Conduct the evaluation SOON after the completion of the course.
3. Keep the evaluation simple.
4. Support the written evaluation with follow-up interviews, if possible. A random sample of course participants called on the telephone may add additional insight and information.
5. Provide an "open forum" on-line for a few weeks after the course is completed for students to engage in a discussion on the strengths and weaknesses of their on-line experience.
6. Include a variety of ways for the students to return the evaluation, such as e-mail, fax, and snail mail.

Once you have tabulated the course evaluations and summarized the comments gathered from interviews and the on-line forum, spend time reflecting on them. Engage in discussions with peers and co-instructors regarding the course evaluations. When you are convinced a change needs to be made, do it!

Making Your Course Visually Appealing and Accessible

The look and "feel" of an on-line course can be as important as the content and skills it is expected to communicate. A study conducted by researchers at the University of British Columbia (R. Boshier, M. Mohapi, G. Moulton, A. Qayyum, L. Sadownik, and M. Wilson, 1997) examined 127 courses taken over the World-Wide Web and evaluated them according to how a student enrolled in each course might respond. "We paid attention to the feeling and tone of the course, not just the content and teaching processes," said Roger Boshier, a professor and leader of the study. It was concluded that appearance "can make or break" an on-line course. Considerable more research is needed in this area, however, it is safe to say, we must pay attention to the visual appeal and "feel" of our course if we expect to maximize student learning on-line."[21]

How do you create an "on-line experience" that grabs your students' attention, offers them a good time and provides a quality learning experience-all at the same time! To add to this mix, some additional variables must also be considered: some students are visually impaired, some have small monitors, some have big monitors, some will use their TV sets to view your course, some will have slow modems and some will have T1 connections. All of these factors come into play as you think of the design and layout of your course.

Design Principles for On-line Courses

If you have selected a commercial courseware package in which to develop and deliver your course, you will be presented with many predetermined format and navigational features. For example, all of the screen illustrations provided in this book were taken from courses developed in the courseware package, Lotus Notes LearningSpace. Many of the design and navigational options in *LearningSpace* are pre-established and can not be altered. However, *LearningSpace* does allow the course developer to customize, to a large extent, the "look" of the page. For example, when designing a course for a university, the university colors and logo could become prominent features of each of the screens in the course. A corporation, to give another example, could display a company logo, trademark or tag line on each screen. Regardless of whether you select a commercial courseware package to customize to your course and institution's specifications, or create your own software and web-page from scratch, you will need a fundamental understanding of what constitutes good design on-line. It is highly recommended that you collaborate with a designer if you are not skilled in the design area. Designing visually appealing on-line pages is an art. In spite of this warning, here are a few suggestions to start you in the right direction.

Fonts

Times Roman and Helvetica (Arial) are the two standard and often used fonts for web-based courses. These fonts are easy to read on-line and withstand the trip from your home computer to the on-line browser. New fonts are created all the time, so keep an eye out for them.

White Space

White space is defined as the space between visual elements. It is a very important part of the total visual image projected to the reader. White space can tell a student where one section ends and another begins. A consistent and systematic use of white space can make your text easy to read and provide smooth transitions from one concept to another-thus increasing comprehension.

Keep it Simple

An on-line page filled with vast amounts of text simply does not work. The same goes for a page which is loaded with graphics. Whenever possible, lecture notes should be organized into concise points, making use of graphic organizers or bulleted key concepts. Lengthy lecture notes, if appropriate and necessary, should be provided in print format. If you expect your students to print out lengthy text-filled pages, permission to do so should be given, as well as instructions on how to print. Inserting simple graphics to break up a page (keeping in mind that graphics take longer for the student to download) also creates a more visually appealing screen.

In addition to the simplicity of the text, the background you select for your pages also plays an important role in visual design. A complicated, 'busy' background does not enhance the visual appeal. Simplicity and consistency are key.

Entire Site Should "Work"

Just as a book cover creates a "look" for a book, so must your on-line pages have an eye appealing appearance that matches its inside. Use a metaphor such as a museum, magazine, school, classroom or city to visually organize your course. This creates an easily recognizable organizational scheme that adds interest and visual appeal. Selecting a theme such as school colors, logo, or ad tag line works well also. The key here is to be both subtle and consistent.

Create a Visually Welcoming Look

Information About the Instructor

Your students want to know who you are. They want to know who is responsible for the content. They want to know what institution is sponsoring the course. Be clear and up front with this information. It is recommended that you provide a photograph and information about yourself as a formal way to "meet" your students. Recall the screen you saw in the beginning of this book in the section entitled, "About this Book?" That screen demonstrates how an instructor can introduce himself or herself in an on-line course. **Display 8B** is another example of an instructor introducing himself to his students at a distance.

Display 8B

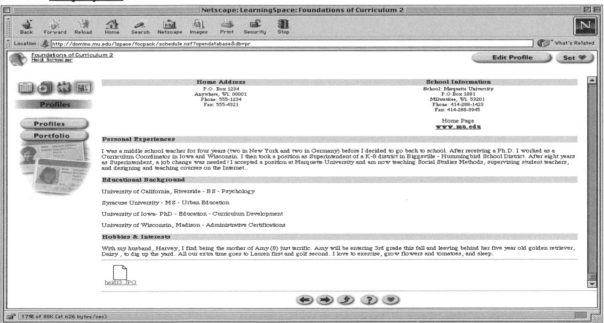

Splash Page

The splash page is that first page students encounter when entering your course. It may be the university's web page or a specially designed page just for your course. Whatever the case, this page should provide clear entry into your course and should load quickly. Your students should be able to easily find their way around the course from this page. Buttons that lead to course outcomes, the required modules or units, assignments and assessments should be clearly visible to direct and guide the student. **Display 8C** is an example of the "splash page" for the courses offered on-line at Marquette University.

Display 8C

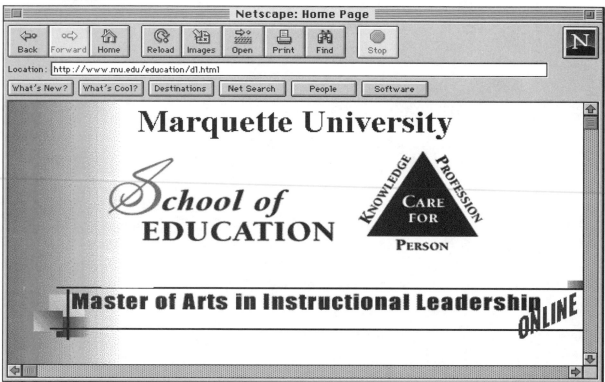

Easy Exit

No one likes to be caught in the corner with no way out! Provide options for easily exiting your course. As students navigate your on-line course, buttons, icons or "exit signs" should be visually available for students to click on to either return to a homepage, or exit the course entirely.

If you are interested in further exploring the design of your on-line course, you may want to check out the <u>Creating Killer Web Sites</u>, by David Seigel. This book is of the most comprehensive resources for designing on-line pages available today. It was the first true design book for the web and became a best seller in 1996. It demonstrates, in very practical ways, how to design for the web.

Summary

Your final two spins, course evaluation and visual design, are two areas of your course that you will not want to leave out. They are critical components for the success of your course.

Course evaluations provide invaluable information and student insights as to how your course could be even better. A carefully designed evaluation that asks the questions you want answers to is yet another demonstration of your willingness to create a rich, interactive student-centered learning environment.

The visual design of your course can be as important as the information contained within it. Pay considerable attention to how your course looks and feels on-line. Ask the design expert for help. After spending considerable time creating a robust, pedagogically sound course, don't ignore the package in which it is presented! Make it visually appealing, welcoming and easy to navigate.

 It's Your Turn!

Evaluation

What will be included in your course evaluation? What questions will you want to ask your students? Perhaps you already use an evaluation in one of your face-to-face classes. If so, go back and take a look at this tool. You may find that with a few changes, it will be appropriate for your on-line evaluation. If not, you may find it helpful to look at the sample evaluation that is located in Appendix 9 of this guide for ideas as you prepare to write your own course evaluation.

Course Design

What special details will you add to your course to make it appealing and welcoming to students? What special touches can you apply to customize it to make it YOUR course? Jot down your ideas. Then draw a sketch of what a screen might look like in your course.

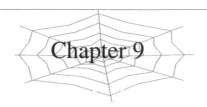

Chapter 9

What Do the Experts Say?

Over the past four years, as I traveled across the United States training those interested in developing and teaching on the World Wide Web, I was frequently asked questions about teaching and learning on-line as people accepted the challenge of embracing a new way of learning. As a summary chapter for this book, I believe it useful to present both a list of the most "frequently asked questions" as well as some reliable and useful answers. To broaden the scope of the answers, I posed the questions to three experts in the field of Distance Learning: Dr. Jerry Patterson, University of Alabama, Birmingham; Jill Rossiter, President of the Management Education Institute; and Dr. Richard Schafer, University of Wisconsin, Learning Innovations.

Following are the "frequently asked questions" and a carefully constructed response for each which reflect, when appropriate, a consensus opinion or view of the three experts. When divergent opinions arose in response to the questions, the difference was noted. The questions are organized by categories: **Curriculum Development**, **On-line Students**, **On-line Instructors**, and **Administration and Fiscal Issues**.

To begin, a synopsis of the educational background and experience of the three respondents is provided.

The Experts

Dr. Jerry Patterson

Dr. Jerry Patterson currently serves as Associate Professor in Educational Leadership, University of Alabama at Birmingham. In his more than 27 years in education, Dr. Patterson has been a high school teacher, elementary principal, curriculum coordinator, assistant superintendent and superintendent. He has conducted workshops for groups throughout the world.

Dr. Patterson began his on-line career in 1997 when he wrote a proposal to implement the first on-line course in the School of Education at the University of Alabama at Birmingham. The proposal was approved and the rest is history. Dr. Patterson currently teaches all of his graduate courses on-line.

Jill Rossiter

Jill Rossiter is President of the Management Education Institute in Indianola, Iowa, a training and consulting firm specializing in boosting employee productivity and leadership effectiveness. A seasoned educator, speaker, and writer, she is a former Associate State Director for the Wisconsin Small Business Development Center. She has also held positions as Associate Academic Dean and Assistant Professor of Management and Education at Simpson College (Iowa) and Assistant Professor of Management at Mankato State University (Minnesota). Rossiter has been involved in the development and teaching of distance education in association with the University of Wisconsin Small Business Development Center; University of Wisconsin Learning Innovations, and Marquette University. Jill became involved in teaching on-line when she administered a grant offering small business courses via the internet at the University of Wisconsin/Extension Small Business Development Center in 1994.

Dr. Richard Schafer

Dr. Richard Schafer is Director of Training Development, UW Learning Innovations, University of Wisconsin, Madison Wisconsin. As Director of Training Development, Dr. Schafer provides leadership and training for course development on the WWW. He creates partnerships with public and private organizations and institutions interested in on-line training and instruction. Dr. Schafer has been a high school teacher, principal and private consultant before returning to the university to play a key role in the organization and marketing of UW Learning Innovations. Dr. Schafer, a learning scientist, became involved in teaching and learning on-line when he was challenged to adapt quality face-to-face teaching to the on-line environment.

The Questions

Curriculum Development

Q How much of a "techie" do I need to be to design and teach a web-based course?

A It helps to be somewhat comfortable with computers and the World Wide Web, but one certainly does not need to be a technological wizard to design or teach a course on-line. As with any unfamiliar software, there is a learning curve involved; but most people should be able to learn the basics (word processing, cutting and pasting, creating attachments, and importing) within a short period of time. A higher level of technical skills is needed to integrate some of the more advanced audio-visual options into your course; however most institutions or businesses have staff to help in these areas.

Q How much up front time needs to be invested in the design of a quality web-based course as compared to the time needed to develop the same course for a face-to-face format?

A The answer to this question varies depending on whether the on-line course was adapted from a pre-existing course/training or whether it was developed "from scratch." In general, the rule of thumb is that more time is needed for the development of on-line courses, with the vast majority of that time being "up front" or prior to the course even beginning. One instructor estimated that it took 40 percent longer the first time he developed a course for on-line delivery and about 20 percent longer thereafter. The increase in time is due to the fact that considerable attention must be paid to clearly outlining course expectations, detailing course activities, discussions and assignments, creating assessments and rubrics, and in general, making the course easy to navigate. This all takes considerable time. In the on-line teaching world, preparing the night before for the next day's lesson is no longer an option. Instead, considerable attention must be paid up front to details that in a face-to-face setting would occur spontaneously with little or no planning. Finally, it is wise to plan for time to "field test" the course to catch any annoying technical glitches or confusing on-line directions.

Q Does the course developer(s) need to be the course instructor(s) and vice a versa?

A It can work both ways. If the course developer is the course instructor, this is the ideal, but by no means a requirement. The course development can be accomplished by someone other than the course instructor, if the development team constantly communicates in both phases: development and instruction.

Q Are there certain courses that can not be effectively taught on-line?

A There are not many limitations, although some courses, such as those requiring lab work or teacher observation of group or individual activities may need to combine on-line instruction with some face-to-face or video-conferencing. Courses that emphasize speaking skills, live-group interaction skills, and nonverbal communication (i.e. counseling) may not lend themselves to on-line instruction without significant adaptations. Some people will tell you that any course can be adapted to the on-line environment and cite an on-line dance course developed at the University of Wisconsin, Madison as an example.

On-line Students

Q What is the most common problem or concern on-line students raise?

A At the start of the course, there are always students with technical problems. It helps to have a technical support team available to answer questions. Another concern has to do with clearly defined course expectations and due dates for assignments and discussions. If students get into trouble in an on-line course, it is typically because they get behind in discussion requirements or project assignments. Learning on-line takes considerable self-discipline and organization. Students need to be encouraged to complete course requirements at regularly scheduled times throughout the week. Two final concerns students have expressed are the lack of spontaneous discussion and missing the face-to-face interaction with other students. As the technology continues to develop, lively, synchronous conversations that more closely resemble a face-to-face discussion will become the norm.

Q What is the most positive aspect of web-based learning from a student's perspective?

A Students like the idea of on-line courses being adaptive to individual schedules, both on a daily basis and over the entire term. Based on the student survey conducted, a majority of the students said that an on-line course was more efficient in the use of their own time. In addition, on-line courses provide a higher level of accessibility to programs otherwise unavailable. Web-based learning truly gives students many more educational options.

Q What are the demographics of your typical on-line student?

A To date, all of my students have been adult learners, the majority of whom work full time, or people in professional or support positions seeking work-related, non-credit training for professional development. The typical age range is from 30 – 50 years old. About half of my students commute at least 45 minutes one way to class. The research is beginning to show that more and more students living on-campus are also opting to take some of their classes on the web as they too are faced with balancing work schedules, class schedules and community service schedules.

Q Is there a certain type of student that shouldn't take a course on-line?

A In each class I have taught on-line, I have had one student who seemed overwhelmed by entering their text information in the "correct" places and being able to assume the "take charge of my own learning" attitude that is necessary for a successful on-line student. On-line learning is a form of independent learning and it takes initiative and persistence to succeed, especially if there are technical problems to aggravate the learning process. Although many students struggled at the outset of the course, virtually everyone became accustomed to the routine after a couple of weeks. In rare instances, however, a student will not be able to grasp the basic concepts, skills and dispositions required to function in an on-line environment. In addition, students who rely on being extremely verbal (translated: they talk too much) have a difficult time trying to "talk too much" on-line. Their verbal overkill becomes conspicuous on-line, and they seem to be even more quickly "dismissed" by their on-line colleagues in this setting than they are during face-to-face classes.

On-line Instructors
Q How much training does it take to be an on-line instructor?

A There are actually two distinct areas in which an on-line instructor needs training: the mechanics of teaching on-line (technical aspects of the courseware being used) and the pedagogy of on-line teaching. Depending on the software package being used, the first dimension of training could be completed in a 1–3 day workshop. Teaching teachers how to facilitate on-line discussions, provide adequate student support and encouragement, administer assessments and furnish meaningful feedback, and, in general, manage the logistics of their on-line classroom requires an additional 2–3 days. We just completed a week training in these two areas for nine on-line instructors and the feedback we received was that the time spent in training was worthwhile and necessary. The worst thing you can do is to ask someone to teach on-line, show them a few basics, and then let them go. Teaching on-line requires excellent teaching skills in general, plus the skills to create a dynamic, highly interactive, well-managed on-line environment.

Q Do students learn as much (or more) in an on-line course than they would in the same face-to-face course?

A Based on the survey conducted, 92 percent of the students felt that the on-line course was more effective in developing higher order thinking skills. In addition, students were asked the following question: "As you consider the teaching/learning dimensions and the responsiveness to student needs, what overall assessment would you give to this on-line course in contrast to traditionally taught courses? You have ten points to spend. Distribute the points in the manner that best reflects your overall assessment of this on-line course relative to traditionally taught courses." The average mean score was: on-line course 7.5; traditional 2.5 points. Also, based on my experience in teaching a group of students face-to-face, then teaching the same group on-line, I can say with confidence that the quality of learning during on-line instruction is at least as strong as face-to-face. How much students learn is a function of the design of the course, the skills of the instructor, and the motivation of the student. So, do they learn as much in an on-line course? They certainly can!

Q Will it take more of my time to teach on-line than face-to-face?

A I estimate that the first course on-line took about 40 percent more time to develop and teach. By the second course, I spent about 20 percent more time. I believe that the additional 20 percent can be attributed to the amount of time spent interacting **individually** with students and their work.

Q Do you lose the ability to really get to know your students in an on-line class?

A I think the teacher has the responsibility to draw out students, whether in the face-to-face classroom or a web-based classroom. Sometimes we are successful and sometimes we are not. I have been amazed at how much personality comes out of students over web-based courses through their personal profiles, discussions, and assignments. I believe it is possible to really get to know your students, even if you have never seen them in "real life." When you think about it, in an on-line course, you are interacting individually with every single person in your course several times a week. How often does that happen in your face-to-face classes?

Q What is an optimal on-line student teacher ratio?

A This may depend on the course; but a course that is structured as highly interactive with considerable time devoted to on-line discussions, projects and assignments to which the instructor is expected to respond in a thoughtful and timely fashion, a ratio of 15 students to 1 instructor is optimal for a graduate level course; 25 students to 1 instructor for an undergraduate course.

Q Does teaching an on-line course equate to the same teaching responsibilities when teaching the same course face-to-face? Explain.

A I taught the on-line version of a graduate course, utilizing the same assignments as I did when I taught the course face-to-face. With my on-line class, I did MUCH LESS didactic teaching and MUCH MORE facilitating. One important note should be added. On-line teaching may need to be more flexible, since technical difficulties can occasionally hamper student progress.

Q How do you give/monitor a test on-line? Will students cheat?

A I do not use actual tests in either my face-to-face classes or my on-line classes. I require papers, discussions and project assignments as performance assessments. Therefore I don't worry about cheating.

Q What are instructor's most positive comments about teaching on-line?

A In my experience, on-line courses are much more responsive to the needs of the student (our customer) without diminishing the quality of instruction. Instructors and institutions need to confront how much they value being responsive to the customer. The answer to this question will begin to drive the decision about offering on-line instruction rather than exclusively offering face-to-face instruction. In addition, teaching on-line offers instructors flexibility, just as it does students. An added bonus to teaching on-line is that our students have the potential of coming from all over the world—this diversity of students and variety of student experiences can make the course very exciting and enriching.

Q What are instructor's main concerns about web-based courses?

A   One concern I have is student attrition—whether due to technical frustration or lack of motivation or self-discipline I become concerned when a student is not successful in my class. If an on-line student doesn't respond to your offers to help, you are limited in what you can do (phone, e-mail, fax, letter).

One respondent wrote: "Although I enjoy teaching on-line, it isn't as much fun for me personally. I happen to enjoy the interaction, spontaneous flow of discourse occurring in face-to-face instruction, and the joy of being with people as a learning community in real-time."

Administration/Fiscal

Q What are the costs involved in moving courses from a traditional face-to-face setting to web-based?

A When putting a course or program on-line, the following costs must be considered: courseware and hardware (both servers to host courses as well as computers for instructors and possibly students); technical support (including server administration and student/faculty support); curriculum development time; class size; student management (registration, add/drop, and so on).

Q Does it cost more to teach on-line?

A This is difficult to assess at this time. Some institutions are charging more for an on-line course to offset the technical costs involved in delivering courses on the web. The very preliminary evidence seems to show that other than the cost of the up front development of courses, it does not cost significantly more to offer a course on-line as opposed to face-to-face.

Q What kind of technical support is needed for on-line courses?

A When designing a course, it is advantageous to have a media specialist who can help with the technical aspects of embedding video, audio and advanced graphics as well as the visual design of the course. After the course is developed and up and running, a person who manages the server and the related software is needed in addition to technical support personnel available to answer both student and faculty questions.

Q What is your biggest challenge in working with faculty new to on-line learning?

A The major challenge can be summarized in the proverbial question, "What's in it for me? Why should I change what I'm doing now when things are working okay?" Many faculty do not see themselves as having customers to serve. The faculty see themselves in the role of giving something (imparting knowledge) to students. Decisions to move to on-line instruction are anchored in customer needs and marketplace viability.

Q Will web-based courses put face-to-face out of business?

A Face-to-face instruction will continue to exist. However, institutions that cling only to this mode of course delivery will find a shrinking market. As universities feel the financial pinch, they will likely re-examine their practices. Web-based courses will allow many more people the flexibility and/or access they need to continue their education, where face-to-face courses could not accommodate them.

Your Web-based Course is Spun!

You are now ready to join the growing number of cyberspace instructors! You have spun a web-based course that is grounded in the most recent research available regarding teaching and learning. Your course is rich in resources and activities that support what is known about multiple intelligences, brain-based research, cooperative learning, and the psychological needs of the learner. You have given serious consideration to what you expect your students to know and do by the end of your course and you have designed assessments and rubrics to objectively evaluate each student's progress. You have thought about your on-line teaching style and you have organized your course to address the concerns and special needs of the on-line learner. Your record keeping system is in place and your technician is hovering nearby! It's time! Have fun!

Appendix 1
Welcome Letter

Sample

Congratulations on being selected to represent your school as a participant in the web-based course entitled: "Survey of Technologies for Instruction, Assessment and Information Management." We are all excited about the course and want to thank you for your willingness to be a real "pioneer" in this endeavor.

Allow me to introduce myself. My name is Heidi Schweizer and I will be one of the instructors for this course. I am an assistant professor at Marquette University in Milwaukee, Wisconsin.

A little bit about myself-I was a middle school teacher for four years (two in New York and two in Germany) before I decided to go back to school. After receiving a PhD, I worked as a Curriculum Coordinator in Iowa and Wisconsin. I then took a position as Superintendent/Principal of a K-8 district in Hartland, Wisconsin. After eight years as Superintendent, a job change was needed. I accepted a position at Marquette four years ago and am now teaching Social Studies Methods, Supervising Student Teachers, and coordinating our on-line courses.

With my husband, Dick, who works for the University of Wisconsin, I find being the mother of Dorothy (8), just terrific. All of our extra time goes to Dorothy first and golf second. I love to exercise, grow flowers and tomatoes, and sleep.

Enough of myself and on to you. Enclosed in this letter is a "Profile Sheet." We are asking that you complete the Profile and bring it to the first class. The information you provide will be included in the "ProfileRoom" of the course. The only people who will be able to access this room will be the students in the class. We are also asking that you bring a photo of yourself. This could be a family photo, a professional photo, a fun photo...whatever you choose. We will be scanning these photos into the ProfileRoom. You can choose not to include a photo, but it does make the course a bit more "personal."

I look forward to meeting all of you. I know that we will have an exciting and interesting learning experience together!

Heidi Schweizer

Assistant Professor

Appendix 2
Verbs According to Bloom's Taxonomy

KNOWLEDGE

know
define
memorize
repeat
record
list
recall
name
relate
state
cite
label
identify
perceive

COMPREHENSION

restate
discuss
describe
recognize
explain
express
identify
locate
report
review
tell
convert
interpret
display
respond

APPLICATION

translate
interpret
use
demonstrate
dramatize
practice
illustrate
operate
schedule
sketch
relate
prepare
show
initiate
influence
express
perform

ANALYSIS

distinguish
analyze
differentiate
calculate
experiment
test
compare
contrast
criticize
diagram
inspect
debate
inventory
question
relate
solve
examine
associate
discriminate
outline
adjust
classify

SYNTHESIS

compose
plan
propose
design
formulate
arrange
assemble
collect
construct
create
design
set up
organize
manage
prepare
combine
compile
develop
integrate
modify

EVALUATION

judge
appraise
evaluate
rate
compare
value
revise
score
select
choose
assess
estimate
measure
weigh
conclude

Appendix 3
Rubric for the Desktop Publishing Project

Criteria
Key: M=Mastery D=Developing   U=Unacceptable

Learning Objectives
____   Use precise verbs to specify expected level of thinking and performance.
____   Address School District Communication Proficiencies.
____   Are Authentic or Performance Based.
____   Address individual differences and learning styles.

Content
____   Subject matter is accurate.
____   Applies to current instructional principles, and appropriate assessment practices.
____   Project is appropriate to learning outcomes.
____   Supportive texts or activities are listed.

Design/Presentation Elements
____   Clearly organized layout.
____   Easy to read with appropriate spacing between lines and print size.
____   Graphics are appropriate, clear, proportional, and of good quality.
____   Images, objects, and labels are placed properly. Figures are distinct from the background.
____   Layout and delivery captures interest.
____   No spelling or mechanical errors.

Project Rubric
____   Criteria sufficiently measures the outcomes.
____   Criteria appropriate to level of middle school student.
____   Criteria clearly allows Student/Peer/Teacher assessment.

Appendix 4
Roles and Responsibilities
for Cooperative Group Members

Successful cooperative groups depend on each member taking an active role in assuring the group functions efficiently and effectively with each member "pulling their own weight". There are a variety of ways to help ensure this, one of them ensigning specific roles to each member.

Please read the descriptions of the three (3) different roles the members of your group will assume. Discuss them among your group and decide who will do what. Each member must agree to take one responsibility and each role may have up to two people assigned.

Roles

1.   **Summarizer** - in some of the Modules the **summarizer** will be asked to summarize the discussion for the week and place it in the MediaCenter for all class members to see.

_____   _____

(name)   (name)

2.   **Technician** - when fellow group members run into technical problems, the **technician** will be available for extra assistance, encouragement and advice. The **technician** should be the person with the most knowledge about hardware and software questions, problems with the Internet, or quick fixes. The **technician** will also work with the "Technical Assistant" assigned to the class.

_____   _____

(name)   (name)

3.   **Encourager** - checks on how well the group is functioning. Encourages group members to participate. Informs the instructor of any problems the group is experiencing and helps those that need extra support with a quick e-mail or phone call.

_____   _____

(name)   (name)

Appendix 5
On-line Group Activity

Name that Group

Now, start a discussion with your group in which you come up with a name for your group.

To do this, click on the icon which will take you to the CourseRoom Discussion area:

When you have reached consensus, have the person designated as the "recorder" return to the Schedule and open the next assignment entitled CourseRoom Work Assignment #4 and enter your choice for a group name. Then save and close.

Send the Name-Assignment #4

Now that you have reached consensus on a name for your group, the person designated as the "recorder" for your group should open the CourseRoom Work area and click on the Comment button. Enter your choice for a group name. Everyone in the class will be able to see your group's choice.

Appendix 6
Data Record

Students	Unit 1 Discussion	Unit 1 Assignmt.	Unit 1 Discussion	Unit 2 Assignmt.	Unit 2 Disc. #1	Unit 2 Disc. #2
Group 1						
Kathy						
Sue						
Joy						
Harry						
Leo						
Group 2						
Jeff						
Tom						
Beth						
Cari						
Jackie						
Group 3						
David						
Cindy						
Scott						
Jerry						
Vicki						

Appendix 7
Necessary Hardware and Software

Sample

Our on-line courses require home/work access to the Internet and a computer capable of playing multimedia. This means a computer with enough system memory (16-32 megabytes RAM or more), and a processor fast enough to play movie files. In addition, the hard drive needs to be large enough to save these files if need be. A modem (28.8) is an essential component if you are taking these courses from home or work.

PC: Windows 95 or Windows NT (Windows 3.1 will not work with *LearningSpace* courses)

1. Minimum 486 processor or faster recommended
2. 16 (32 recommended) megabytes of system RAM
3. Sound card and speakers
4. CD - ROM drive
5. VGA or higher-resolution video adapter (Super VGA, 256 color recommended)
6. Minimum 28,800 bps modem

Macintosh: Power PC-based Macintosh-computer running at 100 MHz or higher

1. System 7.5.3 operating system or later
2. 16 MB of RAM with virtual memory turned on (24 MB recommended)
3. 30 MB of available hard-disk space
4. CD - ROM drive
5. Macintosh-compatible monitor (color monitor with Thousands of Colors mode or better recommended.)
6. Open Transport 1.1 or later
7. QuickTime required for inserting QuickTime movies
8. Minimum 28,800 bps modem

Participants will be required to have the necessary computer capabilities and competency with the following tools before proceeding:

1. A web browser - you must have version 4.0 or later of Netscape or IE 4.0 or later
2. Word processor or Notepad
3. Sound player program (often comes with the sound card for your computer)
4. Connection to Internet and e-mail capabilities

Note: NOT AOL as we have found that students who have used AOL (American On-line) as an Internet provider had major technology problems with our courses. There are many Internet service providers available across Wisconsin. Here is a short list of some that have been successfully used: ExecPC, T-NET, TDSNET, Ball Communications, or MPS.

Appendix 8
Course Evaluation

We are happy that you participated in and successfully completed the web-based course *Foundations of Curriculum*. We are now very interested in your opinions, ideas and experiences regarding web-based teaching and learning. Please take a few minutes to complete the following survey. Your responses will be anonymous.

On-line Learning Environment

You are speaking to a friend who is thinking about taking *Foundations of Curriculum* (on-line) next semester and has just asked you what you got out of the course. List the most important things you learned in this course.

We are particularly interested in anything you can tell us about taking a course on-line. List the strategies you believe contributed to your success in this course. (For example, how did you organize yourself, how did you structure your time, how did you go about completing assignments)

Now that you have completed a web-based course, list the personality traits or characteristics you think a student should possess to be successful in a web-based learning environment?

List any ways your thinking about using technology for instruction and assessment changed as a result of this class.

Please indicate on a scalc of onc to five the degree of "helpfulness" each of the following components of the course were to you as a student:

Learner Packet (yellow book of readings)

1.............2....................3..............4.................5
no value   somewhat useful   useful   very useful   significant aspect of the course

Comment:

Discussions in Modules 1 - 4

1.............2....................3..............4.................5
no value   somewhat useful   useful   very useful   significant aspect of the course

Comment:

Projects (2 required)

1.............2....................3..............4.................5
no value   somewhat useful   useful   very useful   significant aspect of the course

Comment:

Sharing of project ideas ("Pulling it Together" and "Sharing Your Project")

1..............2...........................3...............4...................5
no value   somewhat useful   useful   very useful   significant aspect of the course

Comment:

Instructions on-line (in the media center) for use of various technologies (i.e. desktop publishing, animation, etc.)

1..............2...........................3...............4...................5
no value   somewhat useful   useful   very useful   significant aspect of the course

Comment:

How clear were the goals, aims and requirements of the course? Consider both the on-line instructions as well as instructions in the Learner Packet.

1................2.................3................4...................5
Confusing or never stated   Satisfactory   Very clear

Comment:

How well did the instructors motivate you as a student?

1................2.................3................4...................5
Very little   Moderately   Highly challenging

Comment:

Were the instructors' development and on-line presentation of subject matter clear and organized?

1.................2.................3.................4.................5
Confusing   Satisfactory   Very clear

Comment:

Were the instructors responsive to the needs of the students?

1.................2.................3.................4.................5
Seemed not to care   Satisfactory   Exceptional concern

Comment:

Did the instructor create a climate and set circumstances conducive to on-line learning?

1.................2.................3.................4.................5
Little value   Satisfactory   Much value

Comment:

Given the nature of the course, are the workload demands of the course realistic?

1.................2.................3.................4.................5
Too light or too much   Moderately light or excessive   About right

Comment:

If you desired help outside of class, would the instructors be available and helpful?

1................2................3................4................5

Difficult to get help   Adequate   Very helpful

Comment:

Were the grading procedures and criteria clearly communicated at the beginning of the course?

1................2................3................4................5

Not at all   Adequate   Very clear

Comment:

Were you able to easily communicate with other students during the course?

1................2................3................4................5

Not at all   Adequate   Any time I needed to

Comment:

Overall, was this course was relevant to your needs?

1................2................3................4................5

Not at all   Adequate   Very relevant

Technical Quality

The *LearningSpace* format was easy to use:

1................2................3................4................5
Strongly disagree   Mildly agree   Strongly agree

Comment:

The technology and other media were easy to access:

1................2................3................4................5
Strongly disagree   Mildly agree   Strongly agree

Comment:

All equipment and media were in good working order:

1................2................3................4................5
Strongly disagree   Mildly agree   Strongly agree

Comment:

Appropriate provisions were made for learners to access learning at any time:

1................2................3................4................5
Strongly disagree   Mildly agree   Strongly agree

Comment:

Taking this course saved time and travel expense and minimized "lost time."

1................2.................3................4..................5
Strongly disagree   Mildly agree   Strongly agree

Comment:

I have taken an on-line course before: ___ Yes   ___ No

I would take an on-line course again: ___ Yes ___ No

I would recommend an on-line course to my friend: ___ Yes ___No

I would give this course the following overall rating:

1................2................3................4..................5
low   high

Comments:
Feel free to give us any other comments regarding this course:

END NOTES

1. Phillips, Vickie, *Chronicle of Higher Education*, January 1998.
2. Glasser, William, M.D., *Control Theory*. New York: Harper & Row, 1984.
3. Spady, William. *"It's Time to Take a Close Look at Outcome-Based Education"*, Outcomes,(Summer 1992).
4. Portions of this chapter are drawn from the course entitled, *Using Technology for Instruction and Assessment*, developed by Heidi Schweizer, Joan Whipp and Mercedes Fisher, Marquette University, 1997.
5. Goodrich, Judi. *"Understanding Rubrics."* Educational Leadership, (December 1996/ January 1997), pp. 14-17.
6. Ibid
7. Gardner, Howard, *"The First Seven and the Eighth"*, Educational Leadership, Vol. 55, No. 1, September 1997.
8. Lazear, David G. *Seven Ways of Knowing: Teaching for Multiple Intelligences: Handbook of Techniques for Expanding Intelligence*, Skylight, 1991.
9. Perleman, L. J. *School's Out: A Radical New Formula for the Revitalization of America's Educational System*, Avon, 1992.
10. Harper, Georgia. *Fair Use Guidelines for Educational Multimedia*. Conference on Fair Use, 1997.
11. Tsyver, Daniel A. *"Copyright Law in the United States"* Bitlaw (a comprehensive Internet resource on technology). 1996-1997.
12. Sinfosky, Esther, *Off-Air Videotaping in Education*, New York: Bowker, 1984.
13. Tsyver, Daniel A., *"Copyright Law in the United States"* Bitlaw (a comprehensive Internet resource on technology). 1996-97.
14. Carter, Mary E. *Electronic Highway Robbery: An Artists Guide to Copyrights in the Digital Era*, Peachpit Press, 1996.
15. Website, *Copyright Bay*, http://www.nmjc.cc.nm.us/copyrightbay.
16. Johnson, David W., Johnson, Roger T., & Smith , Karki. *Active Learning: Cooperation in the Classroom*, Edina, MN: Interaction Book Company, 1991.
17. Ibid
18. Ibid
19. Fox, S. *"Paradigm Regained: The Uses of Illuminative, Semiotic and Post-modern Criticism as Modes of Inquiry in Educational Technology"*, Educational Technology Publication, 1991, p. 217-239.
20. Harris, Judi, *"Knowledge-Making in the Information Age: Beyond Information Access."* Learning and Leading with Technology, October 1995.
21. *"Best and Worst Dressed Web Courses: Strutting Into the 21st Century in Comfort and Style"*. Distance Learning Education: An International Journal, Vol. 18. No. 2, 1997.